Organizing Academic Colleges

A GUIDE FOR DEANS

By Bret S. Danilowicz and Anne-Marie McCartan

Organizing Academic Colleges:
A Guide for Deans
By Bret S. Danilowicz and Anne-Marie McCartan
ISBN: 978-0-692-92135-7

©2017 by Bret S. Danilowicz and Anne-Marie McCartan
All rights reserved, Published 2017
Council of Colleges of Arts & Sciences
PO Box 8795
Williamsburg VA 23187-8795 USA
www.ccas.net
Printed in the United States of America

To purchase this book, write *ccas@wm.edu*

Cover design by Jean Pokorny
Cover photo by Annie Spratt

Contents

Figures and Tables

Introduction

It's not where you are today that counts.
It's where you are headed.
—*Arthur Lenehan*

E very year, hundreds if not thousands of people move into the position of college dean. In doing so, they inherit the organizational chart for the college,[1] along with its personnel, job assignments, allocation of office space, and reporting lines. Very little has been published about how a new dean might effectively make sense of all that they come into, including how a dean's office is organized and staffed, the tasks under its purview, and how the work of the office can be organized to handle a dizzying array of responsibilities.

Deans' offices vary in the resources at their disposal, the size of their institution, and which responsibilities are handled centrally at the institution and which are handled at the college level. All these things matter. But regardless of resources, personnel, and responsibilities housed within the dean's office, an efficient college operation possesses clear assignments, job descriptions, and referral procedures to handle the myriad of issues and tasks associated with this level of the academic enterprise.

Reorganizing the structure, staffing, and combinations of colleges, schools, and departments has accelerated of late, and leaders in higher education have had little time to study high-impact practices for how to effectuate change successfully. Sometimes the genesis of reorganization is imbedded in the vision a new president or provost brings to their office. In other situations, reorganization arises from a dean's desire to make it easier for faculty to collaborate across programs that are traditionally siloed or to elevate the visibility of certain programs. Academics are generally too busy to conduct their own research on options for reorganization, especially when reorganizations are initiated rapidly by provosts and presidents.

---

[1] A lowercase "c" is used for academic colleges within an institution, and an uppercase "C" is used to refer to a specific college. "Department chair" is synonymous with "department head."

This need for guidance is the fundamental reason we decided to write this book: to offer a guidebook of sorts to provide insights into the theory and practice of college administrative and academic reorganization. We conducted dozens of interviews with deans and we analyzed hundreds of college websites, and thus offer descriptions of "what is" as well as suggestions how to effectively make changes to existing organizational structures.

As mid-level managers within the larger organization, deans would be well advised to ask whether their organizational structure is the most efficacious given this shifting context.

We write the book from the perspective of members of the Council of Colleges of Arts & Sciences (CCAS). Bret Danilowicz is a sitting dean and Anne-Marie McCartan is CCAS's former executive director. CCAS is a professional association that provides ways for Arts & Sciences deans to help their fellow deans. The Board of Directors supported the publication of this book when it realized the paucity of resources on this topic available to member deans.

Although the target audience is deans of arts and/or sciences, deans of other colleges (business, the fine arts, engineering, nursing, and so forth) will also benefit from its findings. New deans will learn about prevalent organizational models and how the work of professional and support staff can be structured. Continuing deans can better understand the processes that should be employed to maximize the chances that changes in organization and assignments will be successful. Finally, provosts will find this book useful as they have occasion to review and consider changes to the structure of the units over which they preside.

The Context for Organizational Change

Numerous conditions in contemporary higher education are instigating organizational structure change. Examples of these conditions include:

- declining state support for public institutions;
- the changing proportion of tenured/tenure-track faculty versus adjunct or contingent faculty;
- fixation on national rankings;
- pressure from students and their parents for job-focused baccalaureate education;
- increased scrutiny by regional accrediting associations, particularly in the realm of documenting student outcomes;
- growth in administrative and staff positions relative to faculty numbers;
- a growing focus on interdisciplinary teaching and research;
- online education, which often requires cross-campus collaboration; and
- focus on pedagogy and student retention.

At some point, pressure from these multiple demands may build to a point that cracks appear in the existing structure forcing a dean to consider whether reorganization is needed. As mid-level managers within the larger organization, deans would be well advised to ask whether their organizational structure is the most efficacious given this shifting context.

From the perspective of an academic dean, there are *three primary levels of organizational structure* to consider when examining reorganization. These levels are roughly ordered by the extent to which a dean has control over the change process:

1. **Operation of their office**
   a. Deploying associate deans, assistant deans, and directors to oversee academic and student-support functions
   b. Assigning the work of staff to support the management functions
   c. Using faculty fellows

2. **Academic work of faculty (i.e., disciplines)**
   a. Determining which disciplines best fit within the college (as opposed to another college in the institution)
   b. Deciding how to group disciplines (e.g., in departments, schools, or programs; which should be separated and which should be combined)

3. **Organization of colleges within a university**
   a. Determining how many colleges are needed to best fulfill the institution's mission (e.g., whether all A&S colleges should be placed into a single college of Arts & Sciences or divided into multiple colleges)
   b. Deciding the geographic boundaries that represent an institution and its colleges (e.g., should a dean of A&S lead and manage academic programs on one or multiple campuses; would a consolidation of campuses be effective?)

Relevant Literature

Despite a fair number of books on the role of deans as managers and leaders, only a few reference organizational issues; we summarize their findings here.

In *Building the Academic Deanship*, Krahenbuhl (2004) addresses "senior staff organization," making the crucial point that one of the first considerations for a new dean is "the quality and character of the staff." Almost any method of organizing a staff will work with good people, but no organizational arrangement will completely offset complications created by individuals who lack basic leadership attributes (competent, trustworthy, and see themselves as facilitators) (p 45).

In the same text, Krahenbuhl further offers a distinction between using a substantive arrangement (by academic cluster) or a functional one (by areas of responsibility) for how staff members are assigned to cover the work of the college. Bright and Richards (2001) offer a different view. They suggest that a dean can consider assigning responsibilities by academic area, by administrative function, and by constituency. The authors acknowledge, however, "most colleges show a hybrid of these three types" (p 70).

A survey of "sub-deans" conducted by an ad hoc CCAS committee of associate and assistant deans in 1989[2] found that of 13 specific tasks listed on a questionnaire, 34 percent of respondents reported they were assigned to all the areas, along with dozens of "special assignments." Likewise, Mosto and Dorland (2014) note that for those deans who have multiple associate deans, position descriptions and clear parameters are important, such as what individual responsibilities are and how information is shared between positions (p 16).

Organization of the Arts and Sciences

One of the results of such a limited body of literature about reorganization is that the CCAS Executive Office often receives queries along these lines: How are Arts and Sciences typically organized within universities? As the largest national organization of Arts & Sciences deans, the CCAS member database sheds some light on this question. A 2014 analysis[3] of the data on hand[4] revealed that of its 500+ member institutions, 320 (67%) organize the Arts & Sciences disciplines within a single college or school (Figure 1.1). The remaining third house them within anywhere from two to five separate units. Differences in organizing the Arts & Sciences are so vast that in the CCAS member database, over 120 different names are used for colleges/schools housing the disciplines within Arts and Sciences (see Appendix A).

320 (67%) [of CCAS member institutions] organize the Arts & Sciences disciplines within a single college or school

As seen in Figure 1.2, private institutions are much more likely (81%) than public institutions (51%) to combine A&S under one roof. This finding may be a function of size as well as institutional type, as many of CCAS' private-institution members are small- and medium-sized institutions.

---

[2] CCAS Newsletter 10 (May/June 1989): 3. Print.

[3] CCAS Newsletter 30 (June/July 2014): 3. Online.

[4] A few issues complicate this analysis. First, although a high percentage of doctoral-research and master's institutions are CCAS members, only a small percentage of the nation's many baccalaureate-oriented institutions are in CCAS. And second, it's difficult to tell from a title alone whether "Arts" includes the fine and performing arts or whether these programs are housed under free-standing schools outside of Arts & Sciences.

FIGURE 1.1

Institutions Organized into Single versus Multi-unit Arts & Sciences

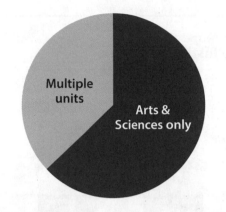

SOURCE: CCAS Newsletter 30 (June & July 2014): 3. Online.

FIGURE 1.2

Public versus Private Institution Organization of A&S

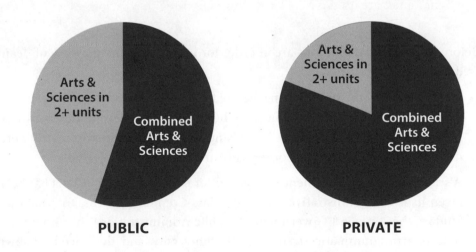

SOURCE: CCAS Newsletter 30 (June & July 2014): 3. Online.

When viewed by institutional type (Figure 1.3), doctoral/research universities are the most likely to have single A&S colleges (68%), followed by baccalaureate and master's institutions (both at 60%).

FIGURE 1.3
A&S Organization by Institutional Type

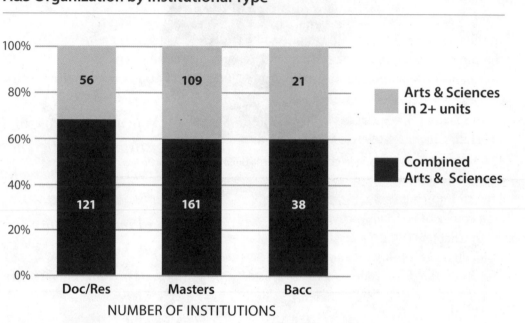

SOURCE: CCAS Newsletter 30 (June & July 2014): 3. Online.

Before proceeding, definitions are in order for units under the purview of deans as used in this book.

- A *department* is the unit housing faculty from a single academic discipline. In smaller institutions, departments may be comprised of several distinct disciplines (e.g., Natural Sciences). There is no attempt at interdisciplinarity here; departments are a matter of convenience and tradition.

- A *school* is often a department so large and/or multidisciplinary that it has been given its own administrative unit (e.g., Mass Communications, International Studies, the Arts, and Government & Public Administration). A school often reflects a programmatic strength of the university, and thus needs its own infrastructure (in advising, development, etc.). One typical rationale of school organization is to encourage teaching and research interdisciplinarity in related fields. This type of school is usually organizationally under a college (e.g., Arts and Sciences), with the administrative head called a director rather than a dean.

- A *college* is the academic unit housing related disciplines, as defined by the institution. Colleges are headed by deans, who report to a provost/vice president for academic affairs. Note: At smaller institutions, occasionally the term "school" is used instead of what more typically is called a college (and is especially true if the institution goes by College rather than University). Some larger universities have held onto using school (instead of college) for historic reasons.

Organization of the Book

In the following chapters, Chapters 2 and 3 address the areas over which deans have the most control: their office. Chapter 2 reports our findings researching the most prevalent models for organizing the dean's office and illustrates each finding with a specific case example written by a dean.

In Chapter 3, we elaborate upon deployingdecanal staff. Chapter 4 offers a framework for assessing the need and potential for making changes to an organizational structure, andChapter 5 describes how to implement organizational changes once the best course of action has been determined.

[W]e acknowledge that every institution is different in its structure, policies, management approach, governance procedures, and in its openness to change.

In Chapters 6 and 7, we address the other two levels of change: below the dean's office (departmental), and above the dean's office (merging or separating colleges and merging universities). In the book's concluding Chapter 8, we offer final summary reflections about deciding if you are ready to make a change, and the most important "lessons learned" from the dozens of interviews we conducted with deans.

As backdrop, we acknowledge that every institution is different in its structure, policies, management approach, governance procedures, and in its openness to change. We write from the perspective of what we have synthesized from our study of this subject over more than two years' time and from what we have experienced ourselves as deans. We hope you find that the data, examples, and narratives make the consideration of college reorganization less intimidating and the process itself more thoughtful and less haphazard.

Organizational Models for the Office of the Dean

Organization isn't about perfection; it's about efficiency, reducing stress and clutter, saving time and money and improving our overall quality of life.

—*Christina Scalise*

Any dean's office holds responsibility for the academic enterprise of the college (the teaching and research done by faculty and learning accomplished by students) as well as for supporting functions not otherwise provided university-wide. By and large, deans have the authority to organize the tasks and personnel as best fits their needs within the resources at their disposal.

Colleges/Schools of Arts and Sciences tend to be the largest and most complex academic units in most non-profit universities–private or public, large or small. Therefore, the models that A&S deans choose for organizing the work of their college varies much more widely than other colleges.

You may wonder if your office (and by "office," we mean the academic personnel and service functions you oversee) is configured optimally to meet your needs and to take advantage of the talents of those working for you. You may ask about what your options are for reorganizing your operation. What models exist? What are the strengths and challenges of each model?

We identified five models (some with variations) most frequently used to organize the operations and personnel under the purview of the dean, based upon our review of several hundred websites to determine the most prevalent models of Arts and Sciences colleges. Our review focused on the size and scope of the college/s of Arts and Sciences, the structure of the dean's office, and how academics are organized.

The models are as follows:

MODEL 1: **Traditional**
                Variation: Traditional + Schools
MODEL II: **Dean-Only**
MODEL III: **VPAA/Dean of the College**

MODEL IV: **Functional + Division Deans**
>   *Type A: Functional + Portfolio Division Deans*
>   *Type B: Functional + Line Division Deans*

MODEL V: **Functional + Administrative Associate/Assistant Deans & Directors**

In this chapter, each model is described more fully and an organizational chart indicating the flow of academic accountability is offered. Support such as staff positions are centralized within the dean's office unless otherwise noted. In the organizational charts, details such as specific titles, presence of associate and/or assistant deans, number of departments, and the like, will vary among colleges using the model. For each model, we list several examples of A&S colleges that use that model and include a case example provided by a CCAS member. The case example will allow the reader to see how a specific model functions and the extent to which it works well from a fellow dean's perspective.[1]

MODEL I: Traditional

This is called the traditional model because it is the most prevalent. Faculty have historically organized themselves into disciplines and governed themselves in departments, led by a chair or a head who reported to a dean. The dean likely had a secretary who kept his or her calendar, typed letters, and organized the filing system.

The number of decanal staff grew over the years, adding to the number of direct-reports to the dean. With expanding enrollments, responsibilities, accountability requirements, and enhanced technology, deans added assistant deans and associate deans to handle the academic workload and professional and classified staff to support the operations of the college. As deans' workloads increased, they may have divvied up liaison responsibility for departmental matters to associate deans while still retaining authority for hiring, tenure, and promotion decisions.

In this model, assistant and associate dean(s) have functional responsibilities (e.g., academic affairs, academic advising, research and grants) and serve as a member of the dean's staff. Operational functions such as finance, communications, IT, human resources, and grants management are usually each staffed by one person who reports directly to the dean.

---

[1] A note about the important issue of the dean's role in the promotion, tenure, and review process. After first attempting to include this within our models and case examples, we concluded that the wide variation among institutions—even within the same model—meant that it was foolhardy to draw generalizations. Within the traditional model, for instance, decisions about P&T may rest squarely within departments in one place, while at another college using the same organizational model, departmental recommendations may be reviewed and contravened by the dean, a collegewide or university committee, the provost, and even (in rare instances) the president or governing board.

FIGURE 2.1
Traditional Model

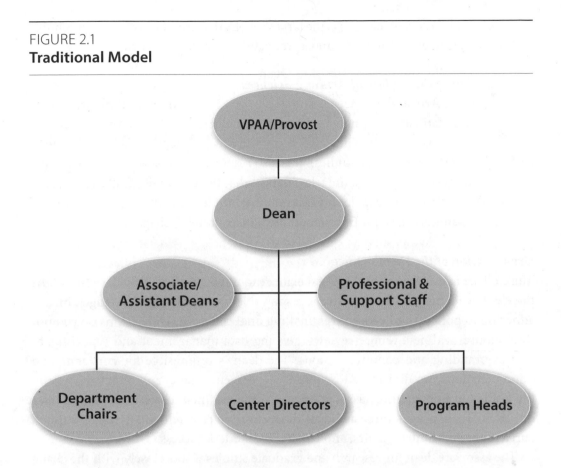

Reporting relationship for academics: Department Chairs → Dean
EXAMPLES: Kansas State University (College of Arts and Sciences); Oklahoma State University (College of Arts & Sciences); Valparaiso University (College of Arts and Sciences); University of Miami (College of Arts & Sciences)

CASE EXAMPLE:
North Carolina Agricultural and Technical, College of Arts & Sciences[2]
From Goldie S. Byrd, Dean

North Carolina Agricultural and Technical State University is a public, land-grant institution located in Greensboro, North Carolina. The Carnegie Classification designates North Carolina A&T as Doctoral Universities - Higher Research Activity. As the nation's largest Historically Black University, the University enrolls over 10,000 students at the undergraduate, master's and doctoral levels. With 38 departments, North Carolina A&T offers 57 undergraduate degree programs with 104 concentrations, 30 master's degree programs with 53 concentrations, and 10 doctoral programs.

---

[2] Since this section was written, the College of Arts and Sciences at North Carolina A&T State University has been split into two units: the College of Arts, Humanities, and Social Sciences and the College of Science and Technology.

The College of Arts and Sciences is the largest of North Carolina A&T's seven schools and two colleges, enrolling 4,074 undergraduate and graduate students.

Organization of the College of Arts and Sciences

The College of Arts and Sciences is comprised of 13 departments (Biology, Chemistry, Physics, Mathematics, English, History, Journalism and Mass Communications, Political Science and Criminal Justice, Energy and Environmental Systems, Sociology and Social Work, and Liberal Studies). It is also responsible for several affiliated units (the learning resource centers, the television studio, the University Galleries, a radio station, the student newspaper, and several other academic centers). Seven Master's degree programs and one Ph.D. program are housed in the College.

Organization of the Dean's Office

The College is led by a dean, three associate deans, and a College Advisory Board. As the chief academic officer, the dean is responsible for overseeing the budget, hiring, adhering to policies and procedures, making final college-level decisions on promotion, tenure, and post tenure reviews, keeping data management and reporting, as well as branding and communications. The dean is responsible for corporate and donor relations, fundraising and alumni engagement. The dean's direct reports on the academic side are three associate deans, 13 department chairs, and three center directors. The College's three associate deans oversee research and graduate studies, curriculum and student affairs, and faculty and student success.

The associate dean for research and graduate studies works closely with the chairs to manage and create new graduate curricula and programs. This dean oversees salaries of graduate teaching assistants and postdoctoral associates and keeps track of research productivity and scholarships in the College.

The associate dean for curriculum and student affairs manages college-level curricular changes, difficult advising issues and issues between students and faculty, and serves as the liaison between the College and other schools and colleges on campus. The associate dean manages college-level committee affairs, the Student Advisory Committee, and provides first-level review of reappointment, promotion, tenure and post-tenure review. Providing college-level support to assure accreditation of five programs in the College is also under the purview of this dean.

The associate dean for faculty and student success manages developmental opportunities for faculty and students; provides oversight for the College's Student Success and Faculty Development Endowment, all alumni-endowed scholarships, all faculty development activities and the College's Innovation Ventures Fund; and designs and assesses undergraduate research training programs, student learning outcomes and faculty development investments.

Ten administrative staff members report to the dean as they provide centralized support services to the departments, including grants management, information technology, assessment, human resources, development, faculty development, and marketing.

Academic Organization

The College's 13 departments are headed by chairpersons who are 12-month employees. They are responsible for managing teaching and advising schedules, student orientations, curriculum development, faculty mentoring, budget development, fundraising, assessment of student learning outcomes, space utilization, faculty and staff workloads, and mediating between students, faculty and parents. Each chairperson is assigned one or two administrative assistants and an associate chair to assist with day-to-day activities, which allows the chair time for his/her professional development.

Strengths and Challenges of This Model

This organizational model, with its associate deans and specialty staff, allows myriad opportunities to plan and create initiatives, strategically using a shared and inclusive approach. Associate deans provide expert advice as well as service supporting many day-to-day and strategic operations of the College. In addition, they are able to provide more individual attention and support to the chairs. The associate deans have the independence and flexibility to create and implement new initiatives, such as our Innovation Ventures Fund, a Global Lecture Series, and the College Endowment. Given the size, breadth and complexity of the College, the associate deans and I are able to attend almost all of the many events among the departments, assist the chairs with special funded and non-funded projects, and assist them with creating external partnerships, in ways that align with their disciplines.

The organization of the College of Arts and Sciences faces challenges in regard to expectations of the University. The College is responsible for instruction for the General Education curriculum. Using a prescribed funding formula for Arts and Sciences disciplines, as well as carrying the highest teaching loads in less expensive disciplines, the College of Arts and Sciences has the smallest operating budget and the lowest-paid faculty at the University. Although it exceeds the University's averages in first-year retention, and four- and six-year graduation rates, it is also expected to be excellent in research, including in disciplines where research funding is minimal.

MODEL I—Variation: Traditional + School

This is the traditional model plus the addition of semi-independent school/s whose directors may have a dotted-line relationship with the college dean. Such an arrangement occurs when a cluster of departments or disciplines achieves a critical mass (of faculty and students) or when a level of external visibility warrants greater autonomy.

The size or stature of these programs may not justify independent-college status, but other imperatives—such as the cross-fertilization of teaching and research interests, a common foundational year for the undergraduate programs, or efficiency of staff and laboratory support—lead to it making sense to house related programs within a larger unit. The dean may also want to signal the range of programs and degrees within this cluster of disciplines. The structure of a "school" may give the programs more prestige and standing among their national peers.

The programs within the school may share other commonalities with the A&S college, such as core requirements for degrees and procedures for promotion and tenure review. In this model, schools are headed by directors who have budget authority and oversee department chairs and program heads, as opposed to schools organized to cluster like disciplines but lack a director with full budget authority or semi-independent status. Occasionally a department becomes named a school due to an agreement with a donor naming the unit. However, such schools functionally remain departments and fall under the Traditional Model.

Typical examples of schools within A&S colleges include Communication Studies, Fine and Performing Arts, and International Studies.

FIGURE 2.2
Traditional + School Model

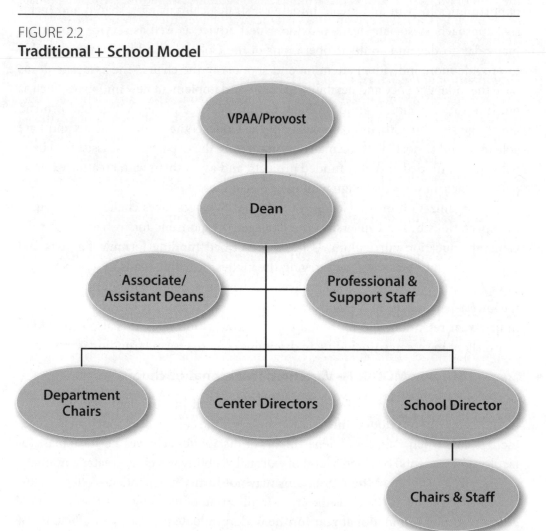

Reporting relationship for academics:

Department Chairs → Dean + Department Chairs → School Directors---→Dean

    EXAMPLES: South Dakota State University (School of Design within the College of Arts & Sciences); Wright State University (School of Music within the College of Liberal Arts)

CASE EXAMPLE:
Texas A&M University-Corpus Christi, School of Engineering and Computer Sciences within the College of Science and Engineering

From Frank Pezold, Dean, College of Science and Engineering

Texas A&M University-Corpus Christi was founded in 1947 as a private Baptist-affiliated institution. Over the years it transformed from an upper-division-only State University to a comprehensive unit of the Texas A&M University System. Located on the Gulf of Mexico, it enrolls more than 12,000 students (including 2,200 in graduate programs). Its Carnegie classification is Doctoral Universities — Moderate Research Activity.

Organization of the School within Arts & Sciences

Arts & Sciences are organized into two colleges: Liberal Arts and Science & Engineering. The latter College fits the model of Traditional + School. Along with its three departments headed by chairs (Life Sciences, Mathematics and Statistics, and Physical & Environmental Sciences), the College of Science and Engineering reorganized its engineering and computer science faculty into a School within the College about eight years ago in response to community pressure to demonstrate a serious commitment to the development of engineering programs that might benefit the local economy.

    The School now enrolls some 1,100 students in eight degree programs, including three graduate degrees, including several that were added after the school was formed. The chairs of the two departments (Engineering and Computer Science) report to the director, but are also in conversation with the dean, and the director reports to the dean as well. Staff within the School include administrative and laboratory support personnel and academic advising. In essence, the School of Engineering and Computing Sciences functions semi-autonomously within the College, although the faculty of the School do meet with the other College faculty. As the College dean, I am part of the review process for promotion and tenure decisions and forward my own recommendation to the provost.

MODEL II: Dean-Only

The Dean-Only model requires little explanation; the dean oversees all academic and support functions not already covered at the institutional level without any associate or assistant deans. Colleges use this model either because of their size (small and manageable) or because the dean chooses to maintain responsibility and authority for all college matters. It is also used when a smaller institution has divided its Arts & Sciences into more than one college and therefore the dean oversees a limited number of departments. In some instances, degrees and programs are organized into academically related clusters rather than departments (e.g., School of Humanities & Social Sciences and School of Sciences) and are headed by a chair or director of that cluster or division.

FIGURE 2.3
Dean-Only Model

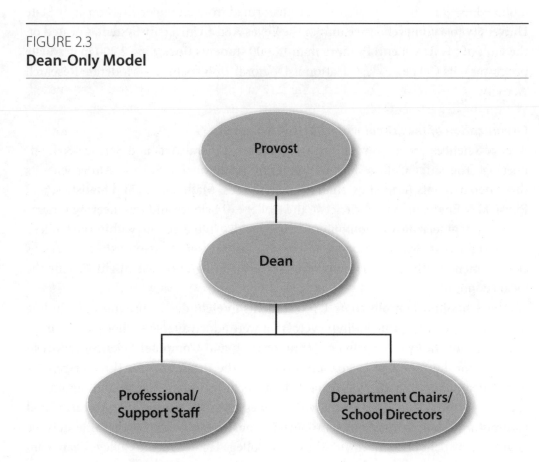

Reporting relationship for academics: Department Chairs → Dean
EXAMPLES: Dakota State University (College of Arts and Sciences); Fort Valley State University (College of Arts and Sciences); Malone University (College of Theology, Arts & Sciences); Ursuline College (School of Arts and Sciences)

CASE EXAMPLE: University of Saint Francis, College of Arts & Sciences
From Robert Kase, Dean

Founded in 1920 by the Sisters of St. Francis as a liberal arts college for women, the University of Saint Francis is a co-educational University today with traditional and professional programs. The original "College of St. Francis" concept of a small liberal-arts undergraduate institution evolved into a separate College of Arts and Sciences as one of four colleges within the University. This urban school resides in the southwestern suburbs of the Chicago metropolitan area and has a large commuter population and a significant graduate online population. Classified by Carnegie as a Master's College and Universities - Larger Programs institution, the 3,500 students are fairly evenly distributed between undergraduate and graduate programs.

Organization of the College of Arts and Sciences

The College of Arts and Sciences (CAS) has one full-time dean, 12 department units (comprised of 3-12 faculty members) with each headed by a chair who receives a one-course load release (3 credits) from a 12 credit [4/4] teaching load per semester. Within the departments that house programs, some have coordinators who report to the department chair. Program coordinators receive either course release or a stipend depending upon the situation.

Academic Organization

All faculty report to the Dean of the College, who supervises and assigns all mentoring of new faculty and in conjunction with the department chairs, oversees all faculty evaluation processes. As a dean without associates, I handle most faculty, staff, and student issues in the College. I address all probation and dismissal issues, appeals, budgeting, personnel, planning, and vision for CAS. I work with the department chairs to resolve all faculty, student, and program issues.

Department chairs normally receive a one-course load release for their service. I have been giving two chairs in the largest departments two-course load releases, but this is not in our policy manual and is at my discretion. Department chairs oversee the assignment of teaching loads, course evaluations, department organization, file assessment reports and plans, hire adjuncts when necessary, and represent their programs to the dean. Some departments are small with 40-60 majors, while others have 180 majors.

Each department has its own departmental budget, and department chairs manage the spending of it. Every departmental expenditure requires the dean's approval, followed by approvals from the Provost/VPAA, Controller, and finally the VP of Finance. This approval process is all done electronically but is quite ponderous.

Strengths and Challenges of This Model

As a dean who oversees virtually everything happening in the College, I feel quite attuned to issues and engagements throughout the entire College. This positive aspect of this model helps me promote CAS endeavors and steer the College, and it helps me in determining future directions and planning. It keeps me engaged with the students and faculty from all disciplines. The challenge of this model, as one can imagine, is that I am pulled in many different directions and it is sometimes taxing to stay on top of it all. Department chairs can make many decisions independent of me, however.

The workload involved in supervising 75 direct reports—not to mention university and student activities in the evenings—often seems untenable. The executive cabinet has offered and even encouraged me to hire an associate dean, but I have chosen instead to use my additional resources for badly needed new faculty hires.

MODEL III: VPAA and Dean of the College

This model was the predominate model for traditional private liberal arts colleges, with the chief academic offer serving as the Dean of Faculty (or Dean of the College). All academic functions (library, advising) and support functions (IT, facilities) might come under the dean's purview, with the VPAA/Dean reporting directly to the president. This model is seen less frequently now as many traditional liberal arts colleges have created a provost's position to handle the increasingly complex requirements of running a college and they have added professional schools with their own deans or directors.

CASE EXAMPLE: *Marymount Manhattan College*
From David Podell, Vice President for Academic Affairs and Dean of the Faculty

Marymount Manhattan College (MMC) is a small liberal arts college serving about 1,800 students. It was originally an urban offshoot of Marymount College in Tarrytown, New York, which closed. Founded as a Catholic women's college by the Religious of the Sacred Heart of Mary, it has been independent and co-educational for several decades. MMC resides on Manhattan's Upper East Side occupying three buildings. Its Carnegie classification is Bachelor's Colleges - Arts & Sciences institution.

Organization of Arts &Sciences
In addition to the VPAA and Dean of the Faculty position, there is an associate dean, an assistant dean, and two administrative assistants. The Division of Academic Affairs oversees all of MMC's academic programs and the resources designed to support the achievement of our academic goals and mission. Thus, all academic departments and divisions report to the Division of Academic Affairs. The College is organized into five academic divisions (some of which contain individual departments, each of which has a chair):
- Business
- Fine and Performing Arts (Art, Dance, and Theatre Arts)
- Communication and Media Arts

FIGURE 2.4
VPAA and Dean of the College Model

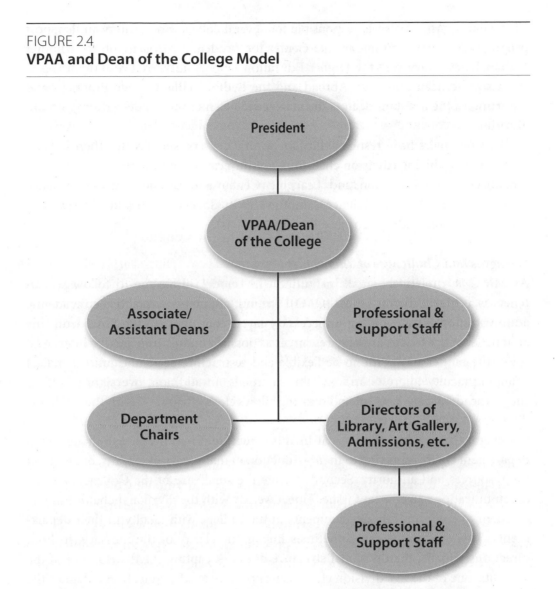

Reporting relationship for academics: Department Chairs & Directors→VPAA/Dean
EXAMPLES: Agnes Scott College; Pomona College; Transylvania University; West-minster College (PA)

- Humanities and Social Sciences (English, International Studies, Philosophy and Religious Studies, and Politics and Human Rights)
- Science (Biology, Communication Sciences and Disorders, Mathematics, and Psychology)

They offer 25 majors and an Interdisciplinary Studies major drawing from various divisions. These divisions report directly to me.

Academic Affairs also is responsible for several collegewide centers and support programs. Reporting to me are the Center for Academic Advisement, the Thomas J. Shanahan Library, and the Higher Education Opportunity Program; reporting to the associate dean are Study Abroad and the Bedford Hills College Program; and reporting to the assistant dean is the collegewide Center for Academic Support and Tutoring.

Division chairs have responsibility for several centers, such as the Theresa Lang Center for Producing (division chair for Communication and Media Arts); the Ruth Smadbeck Communication and Learning Center and Samuel Freeman Science Center (division chair for Science); and the Hewitt Gallery of Art and Theresa Lang Theatre (division chair of Fine and Performing Arts).

Strengths and Challenges of This Model

As MMC is a relatively small institution, this model allows me to follow several tenets as a chief academic officer (CAO): The first of those tenets is to keep academic administration lean, avoiding unnecessary layers that distance the CAO from the action. Second, to focus as many resources as possible on full-time faculty lines. And third, the model allows me to be flexible and restructure academic units to reflect changing faculty interests and enrollment trends. In addition, oversight of offices such as academic advisement and tutoring allows close integration with the academic divisions.

Several drawbacks are inherent in this structure. First, divisional chairs—with department chairs reporting to them—function in many ways like deans, but without the resources and authority. Second, despite the small size of the College, effective communication is a constant issue. I meet weekly with the divisional chairs and rely on them to communicate developments in the College with faculty in their departments. This extra layer can sometimes impair the clarity of the message, in both directions. Finally, the divisional structure does not capture the distribution of the students: one of the five division chairs is responsible for the education of half of the College's students. This unevenness puts the one division chair at a disadvantage in group decision making.

MODEL IV, Type A: Functional + Portfolio Division Deans

This structure is most often found in large research institutions with a single college of Arts and Sciences, where the size of departments and large number of faculty members require an extra layer of oversight and support.

The college dean is likely to have functional associate/assistant deans with responsibility for cross-college issues (e.g., student advising, undergraduate education, space assignments) and to have other associate (or senior associate) deans who have strong liaison responsibilities for a related cluster of departments (usually called divisions). Those chosen to lead a division are likely to be on the faculty in one of the departments within the division. The division heads make recommendations to the dean about hiring, retention, academics, and the major budget, allowing the dean to spend more time on responsibilities such as alumni relations and fund-raising.

A variation of this model is where the portfolio deans also have cross-college (functional) responsibilities in their position descriptions.

FIGURE 2.5
Functional + Portfolio Division Deans Model

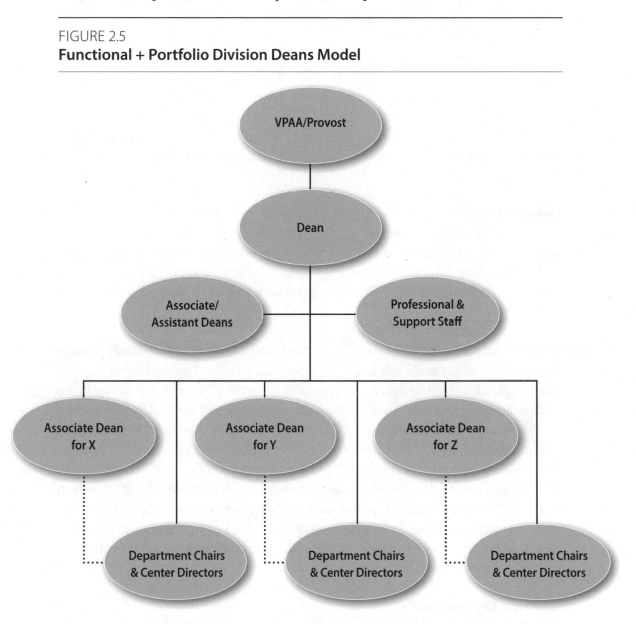

Reporting relationship for academics: Department Chairs ---→ Associate Deans → Dean
EXAMPLES: University of Connecticut (College of Liberal Arts and Sciences); University of Colorado, Boulder (College of Arts & Sciences); Oregon State University (College of Liberal Arts)

CASE EXAMPLE: *University of Delaware, College of Arts and Sciences*
From George H. Watson, Dean

Founded as a small private academy in 1743, the University of Delaware received its charter from the State of Delaware in 1833 and was designated one of the nation's historic Land Grant colleges in 1867. Today, UD is a Land Grant, Sea Grant and Space Grant institution and designated in the Carnegie Classification as a Research University–Highest Research Activity.

A state-assisted, privately governed institution, UD offers a broad range of degree programs: three associate programs, 147 bachelor's programs, 119 master's programs, 54 doctoral programs, and 15 dual graduate programs through seven colleges and in collaboration with more than 70 research centers. The student body encompasses more than 17,000 undergraduates, more than 3,600 graduate students, and nearly 800 students in professional and continuing studies. The College of Arts and Sciences is the oldest and largest of UD's seven colleges.

Organization of the College of Arts and Sciences

The College of Arts and Sciences (CAS) at UD consists of 23 academic departments and 27 interdisciplinary programs and centers serving 7,000 undergraduate students and 1,100 graduate students. We offer 82 majors (including 10 of the 25 most popular majors at UD and 12 of the 25 most popular double majors) as well as 69 minors.

Organization of the Dean's Office

The Office of the Dean is organized by academic and administrative leadership under the direction of the dean, while a College Advisory Council comprised of alumni, academic leaders and business leaders provides a high level of volunteer service to the College and UD, and helps to shape the strategic direction of the College.

The dean is the chief academic officer of CAS, and maintains responsibility for: strategic planning; development and alumni relations; budgetary and faculty/ staff position planning, recruitment, and retention; promotion and tenure recommendations; and mentoring and annual appraisals of department chairs. The dean works actively on collegewide issues such as undergraduate curricula and graduate programs with associate deans and professional staff, and works with the provost, central administration, and deans of other colleges regarding university priorities and planning, advancement, and resource allocation.

Academic Organization

Direct reports to the dean on the academic side include four associate deans, each assigned to disciplinary portfolios:

- the arts (4 departments, programs and centers)
- humanities (20 departments, programs and centers, and secondary education)

- natural sciences (9 departments, programs and centers)
- social sciences (18 departments, programs and centers)

Additionally, a deputy dean serves as a stand-in for the dean and manages several cross-portfolio and interdisciplinary activities. Department chairs and directors of programs and centers, who report to their respective portfolio associate dean, oversee the daily operations of their individual units.

Administrative Support

Direct reports to the dean on the administrative side include: a chief administrative officer, who oversees finance and administration activity; a senior assistant dean, who manages undergraduate academic services for all CAS undergraduate students; and a director of communications, who handles strategic communications planning and public relations for the College. A director of development who resides in UD's central Office of Development and Alumni Relations has a dotted reporting line to the dean.

Strengths of This Model

We have used this portfolio structure in CAS with four associate deans since 2001. I was the inaugural associate dean (AD) of natural sciences, and led the College as dean in this model for more than six years. As both a participant and a leader in the portfolio structure, I find it offers several advantages regarding disciplinary diversity and advocacy, fundraising, daily operations and triage, communications, and succession planning. In particular, the portfolio model offers a clear path forward for longevity and effectiveness of a dean working in the highly demanding and complex arena of a large liberal arts college within a research university.

Disciplinary Diversity & Two-Way Advocacy

First and foremost, ADs provide a level of expertise and disciplinary diversity that as dean, I alone could not provide. They are accomplished scholars and experts in their respective fields and share their knowledge and skills with me as I am the final decision maker in many instances. The ADs also take on a two-way advocacy role, both as stronger advocates for the College by "translating" for the dean and translating "up" from departments and programs to the dean. For example, if the Department of Music or of Art and Design has an initiative, question, or concern, the AD can assist with interpreting the need and value-added in messaging to me. This two-way advocacy is also helpful in promoting interdisciplinary activities and identifying opportunities for collaboration among portfolios.

Daily Operations & Triage

With such a diverse array of departments, centers and programs, there are daily issues and challenges to be addressed. The ADs are essential in triaging day-to-day interactions, working directly with department chairs and program directors to identify solutions to a variety of issues and questions. I routinely ask an AD to join me when I meet with a department chair or director; this extra set of ears in the room facilitates active listening and critical thinking.

Fundraising

Increasingly, the dean's role is one of fundraiser. Meeting with donors takes me out of the office, sometimes for extended periods. With AD leadership, I work externally, meeting fundraising obligations while the ADs work with our development team and alumni in a portfolio, taking on a greater fundraising role.

Communications

Leadership of the ADs is not only an advantage in terms of administrative operations of the Dean's Office and the College; the portfolio structure also enables better messaging in terms of internal and external communications. Through the portfolio structure, we build a stronger identity, both in terms of what the arts, humanities, natural sciences, and social sciences stand for at UD, but also in terms of what experience prospective students can expect. Additionally, the ADs act as content-area experts for press and media interactions instead of the dean being the only leadership respondent. As the largest of UD's seven colleges (and almost four times the size of the second largest college), explaining the College in the context of portfolios helps us manage perceptions internally and the context provides us a stronger voice on discussions ranging from budget models to admissions decisions.

Succession Planning

The AD assignments and portfolio structure act as an excellent model for succession planning. For example, as the inaugural AD for the natural sciences I ran about 40 percent of the College. The experience as a divisional dean was beneficial in making the transition to the deanship. I encourage one-year interim AD appointments, which helps determine a person's fit with the leadership team, as well as manage expectations for what the role entails.

Challenges of This Model

Despite the numerous advantages, organizing the Dean's Office through the portfolio model also presents its challenges, including the following:

Staying Informed

The dean is a conduit to central administration and thus, is regularly the sole recipient of firsthand information. ADs have the responsibility of a dean in many ways, but they are not necessarily empowered to be a part of the process at a central administration level. Therefore, it is critical for the dean to communicate regularly with ADs to ensure priorities and messages are aligned. It takes a significant amount of time to hold weekly one-on-one meetings with the deputy dean and each of the ADs, as well as weekly team meetings (also including the chief administrative officer, budget manager, director of communications, and senior assistant dean for undergraduate academic services), and twice-yearly retreats.

Credit for Work

ADs complete a significant amount of work, much of it essential (e.g., drafting promotion document letters as primary reader of a dossier, evaluating faculty appraisals and materials, peer reviews), but because the dean is the final sign-off or voice, ADs often do not receive visible credit. Public acknowledgement by the dean of AD leadership contributions is an important element of developing and sustaining high performing teams.

Collaborative Requirements

Operating in a portfolio environment, ADs must work collaboratively. If individuals are competitive or territorial over their academic areas, you run the risk of not getting appropriate or adequate representation. The dean must be conscious of this risk and manage appropriately, appointing ADs who have the ability to think broadly, allocate resources fairly, and work well as a member of collegial team.

Ultimately, the benefits of the portfolio organizational model outweigh those of other models of organizing a large and complex college. Myriad demands on academic deans necessitate an effective model of organizing the workflow and decision-making. Associate deans bring valuable disciplinary perspectives as well as diverse experiences and views of the academic landscape. With appropriate attention to the needs of associate deans and their management in this collaborative environment, deans can advance their colleges while maintaining sustainable careers and work-family balance.

MODEL IV, Type B: Functional + Division Line Deans

This model is similar to the Functional + Portfolio Deans model described above, but is distinguished by greater autonomy of the academic divisions and the greater authority of the person who heads a division (called variously senior associate dean, associate dean, division dean, or dean). This organizational structure is most often found in large public institutions.

In this model, division deans are known as "line" officers as they are instrumental in directly promoting the mission of their units and have supervisory responsibilities. By delegation from the dean, they are given autonomy through practice and policy to make decisions. These decisions are not absolute; final sign-off on hiring, promotion, tenure, and the like may still reside with the dean. There is no dotted line from the department chairs to the executive dean. Division deans may have associate/assistant deans and professional staff of their own.

FIGURE 2.6
Functional + Line Division Deans Model

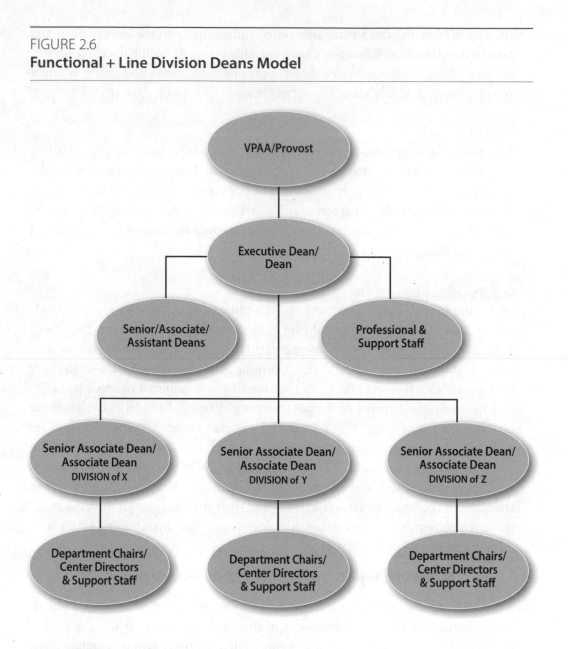

Reporting relationship for academics:

Department Chairs → Division Deans → Executive Dean

EXAMPLES: University of Illinois Urbana-Champaign (College of Liberal Arts and Sciences); University of North Carolina, Chapel Hill (College of Arts and Sciences); Penn State University (College of the Liberal Arts); University of Washington (College of Arts & Sciences)

CASE EXAMPLE: The Ohio State University, College of Arts & Sciences
By David Manderscheid, Executive Dean and Vice Provost

Founded in 1870 by the Ohio General Assembly as the Ohio Agricultural and Mechanical College, the institution received Land-Grant status under the Morrill Act in 1862. Renamed The Ohio State University in 1878, today the main OSU campus in Columbus is the third largest in the U.S. It is designated in the Carnegie Classification as a Research University - Highest Research Activity. OSU has 16 colleges and the College of Arts & Sciences is the largest. All told, the University offers over 200 bachelor's degrees and has 97 master's and 94 doctoral programs. The College of Arts & Sciences delivers over 50 percent of credit hours on campus.

Organization of the College of Arts and Sciences (ASC)

The College of Arts and Sciences at OSU consists of 38 academic departments and schools as well as more than 20 centers and institutes organized under three divisions. Over-900 tenured and tenure-track faculty members (plus over 300 FTE associated faculty) serve 16,000 undergraduate students and 3,000 graduate students. ASC offers over 80 majors and over 100 minors. In addition to serving students on the Columbus campus, ASC is the tenure home of over 50 faculty on four regional campuses (in Lima, Marion, Mansfield, and Newark) who teach in the Arts and Sciences on those campuses.

Organization of the Dean's Office

As Executive Dean & Vice Provost, I lead the College of Arts and Sciences with the support of the vice dean for academic affairs. For many decades, the Arts and Sciences were divided among five colleges. The colleges were brought together in 2010 into a single A&S college. Some vestiges of the legacy colleges were retained, so today ASC is organized into three divisions (Arts & Humanities, Natural & Mathematical Sciences, and Social & Behavioral Sciences), each led by a divisional dean. In addition to them, direct reports to the executive dean include the vice dean, the chief administrative officer, and the heads of a small number of support offices.

   I provide collegewide leadership (heading the College's strategic planning efforts, including setting priorities for the College); oversee academic affairs (making all P&T recommendations to the provost and approval of hiring department chairs and faculty); and approve all curriculum decisions. I represent the College on multiple university committees, along with the other 15 deans and in my position as one of four executive deans. I serve on additional university committees by my vice provost role. The size and nature of OSU, however, often has me focused outward, meeting with donors and alumni.

Academic Organization

The divisional deans are each assigned to disciplinary portfolios and oversee from eight to 21 departments and schools. Department chairs and directors of programs and centers—who report to their respective division deans—oversee the daily operations of their individual units. I set the budgets for the divisions, and the division deans set the budgets for their departments. Division deans make recommendations to me for the appointment of their department chairs. Additionally, all the deans–vice, divisional, associate and assistant–have collegewide functional roles. Each has a responsibility for a cross-college area (e.g., graduate education, research, outreach and engagement) for the entire College.

Administrative Support

I oversee Communications and Advancement (including development and alumni), centralized administrative support within ASC alongside the chief administrative officer (Human Resources and Information Technology), and an associate executive dean for curriculum, instruction, and student engagement (advising & academic services, strategic recruitment & diversity student programs, and curriculum). Additional administration support (e.g., lab technicians) falls under the oversight of the division deans and departments.

Strengths and Challenges of This Model

Given the size and scope of operations, a level of managerial authority between the departments and the executive dean is imperative in order to get things done. The divisional organization structure allows our faculty to feel both closely aligned with those in related disciplines *and* a part of what I have pushed since taking the position in 2013: it is not Humanities vs STEM—it is about liberal arts and the professions, and how we need to maintain the value of what the liberal arts represents. Being "housed" in a single college allows us to live this much more effectively than if we were separate colleges. This ethic is why we don't highlight the divisional structure on our website. We are trying to break people of the habit of thinking of divisions as separate entities rather than as an organizational tool. The single-college structure also helps foster cross-disciplinary and interdisciplinary research and teaching.

As a single A&S college, we have a stronger voice at the University table. We can be the 800-pound gorilla. The challenge of this is that when only one dean per college is at the table, I sometimes have the same voice as a dean of a college with 20 faculty members.

Having division deans with authority means I can face outward, both within and outside the University. With much of the day-to-day business handled by the deans, I contribute to university committees and meetings about central issues. And importantly, along with attending to international partnerships and taking on national leadership roles with professional associations, strong division deans allow me to focus much of my time with constituents outside the university.

Finally, we realize some efficiencies that derive from sharing services across the units. For instance, we have been able to develop the most sophisticated HR operation of any college in the University.

Of course, there are some disadvantages to this model. With this span of disciplines, we are academically heterogeneous. If you try to apply the same set of rules across disparate departments, it does not make sense. One obvious example is that where new hires receive different start-up packages depending upon their field. Promotion and tenure decisions also vary across departments. We handle typically around 60 P&T cases in any year, which is simply too many to ask one faculty panel to handle. Thus, the College has one set of standards but three different panels (one for each division) which conduct reviews. When the recommendations come to me, I ensure the College standards are applied across the divisions.

In a day-to-day reality of over 1000 faculty, close to 20,000 students and over 2,000 staff, I rely heavily on my divisional deans. Often times, however, an issue will arise that goes up the chain from faculty member to chair to division dean to me. My challenge in such cases is knowing enough about the individuals involved to make a decision.

Another issue that often needs discussion is: Who's in charge of what? As a college, we are only six years old and our structure evolves. For example, at one point each division had its own associate dean who handed faculty matters, which led to inefficiencies. This was illustrated one day by a call I received from a vice provost. She reported to me that one of our associate deans had phoned her with a straightforward question about P&T. She wondered why the person had not asked another associate dean. Over time we have become more cross-functional with each divisional dean and the associate and assistant deans tasked with some collegewide responsibilities and expertise. Likewise, I added a new vice dean to handle all faculty affairs across the College. These changes were made in the last few years so we spend less time on occasion asking ourselves, "Who should do this?" But the advantage is we are all talking to each other and the College evolves to a more effective structure.

MODEL V: Functional + Administrative Associate/Assistant Deans & Directors

Two distinct types of personnel distinguish this model: positions reporting to the dean in academic and support arenas, and line positions overseeing major operational functions. The administrative head of these operational units may be an associate or senior associate dean (for academic functions) or a director (for support functions). Such a structure is used due to the size and complexity of the institution and its colleges and because the dean wishes to retain direct oversight of departmental matters (through the chairs).

Extant in public and private institutions, this model is found in major research universities that house all Arts and Sciences under a single college (although there are instances in split A&S colleges, e.g., Arts & Letters or Natural Sciences, which also utilize this model). The dean directly oversees his/her own academic and support staff members (along with the associate deans with administrative responsibility) and retains direct oversight of departments and programs (although associate deans may be assigned liaison responsibility).

FIGURE 2.7

Functional + Administrative Associate/Assistant Deans & Directors Model

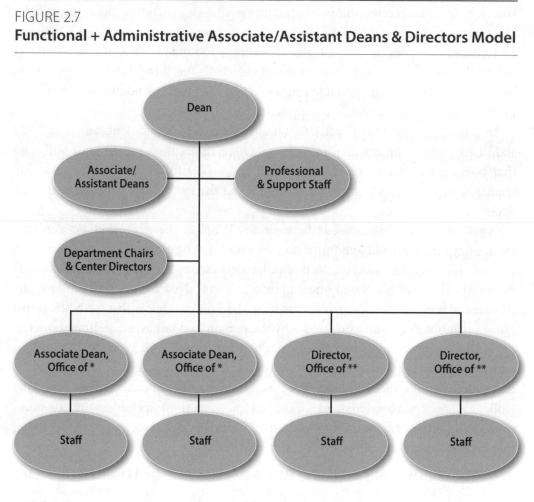

* Office of _____ (e.g., Undergraduate Studies; Graduate Studies; Academic Programs; Budget & Finance)

** Office of _____ (e.g., Development; Finance; Technical Services; Advising; Communication; Business Affairs)

Reporting relationship for academics: Department chairs → Dean; Administrative Associate/Assistant Deans & Directors → Dean

EXAMPLES: Texas A&M University (College of Liberal Arts); University of Illinois at Chicago (College of Liberal Arts & Sciences); North Carolina State University (College of Sciences); George Washington University (Columbian College of Arts & Sciences)

CASE EXAMPLE: *University of Kentucky, College of Arts & Sciences*

From Mark Kornbluh, Dean, and Kirsten Turner, Chief of Staff and Assistant Dean

Founded in 1864, the University of Kentucky is the Commonwealth of Kentucky's flagship Land Grant institution. Designated in Carnegie as a Doctoral University - Highest Research Activity institution, the university is dedicated to improving people's lives through excellence in education, research and creative work, service and health care. With approximately 2,200 faculty and more than 12,500 staff, the university's total enrollment is almost 30,000, with 22,000 undergraduates and 8,000 graduate students and postdoctoral scholars.

Organization of the College of Arts and Sciences

The College of Arts and Sciences is one of 17 academic colleges. It consists of 18 academic departments and more than two dozen interdisciplinary programs and centers. Its annual operating budget of more than $70 million supports 440 faculty and 200 staff. The faculty in the College of Arts and Sciences teaches more than sixty percent of the university's undergraduate general degree requirements and has some 5,000 undergraduate majors and 1,000 graduate students and post-doctoral scholars.

Organization of the Dean's Office

In an institution as large as the University of Kentucky, academics can easily become mired in bureaucracy. We believe faculty should spend their time on the philosophical underpinnings and vision of their work, and college staff should be empowered to help them navigate the bureaucratic structures that could impede their work. Thus, the College's driving philosophy is that academic decisions must undergird everything we do, including the College's administrative structure. Faculty governance is paramount at the College, and thus the College's administrative mission is simply *to enable the work of the faculty and students*. We have focused all College operations on how to help the departments, department chairs, and faculty achieve our collective and their individual goals.

For example, department chairs were previously responsible for their facilities and physical plant—something for which most had little or no expertise. To help them, we hired a retired Air Force ROTC commander who is now the director of space and facilities and has a team of people working *for* the department chairs. Management of all College facilities is centralized, and staff members assigned to these tasks know their primary function is to enable the departments.

Our senior leadership team consists of five associate deans who come from the faculty to serve on three-year renewable appointments. Also included in the senior leadership is a chief of staff position who carries the title of assistant dean. The chief of staff has two purposes: to serve as a confidential advisor to the dean and to oversee all the staff units (non-academic) in the College, which comprises some 185 employees.

Academic Organization

The five functional deans are:

- Senior Associate Dean of Faculty
- Associate Dean for Undergraduate Programs
- Associate Dean for International Affairs
- Associate Dean for Advising (with direct supervision of academic advisors).
- Associate Dean of Research and Graduate Studies

The department chairs report to the dean, although they are free to consult the appropriate associate dean on specific issues. A Council of Chairs meets every two weeks and is structured to be interactive. It serves as the dean's primary sounding board (outside of the senior leadership) for policy issues and the future direction of the College. The dean also uses an Executive Committee, comprised of six elected tenured faculty members, as a sounding board for topical issues. The Executive Committee meets once a month throughout the academic year and often in conjunction with the Council of Chairs. We also have two advisory boards: a National Strategy Board and a Development Council.

Administrative Support

In addition to the service offices listed under Academic Support, other offices within the College are:

1. Space and Facilitates (headed by a director)
2. Finance and Administration (headed by a director)
3. Human Resources (headed by a director)
4. Creative and Technical Services—The HIVE (headed by co-directors)
5. Development (headed by a senior director)
6. Project Management (headed by a director)
7. Enrollment Management and Decision Support (recently promoted to assistant dean)
8. Staff Support (headed by a director)

These offices report to the chief of staff, who works closely with the dean in a team approach.

Strengths and Challenges of This Model

The size and scope of our operation requires clear organization. Centralizing support functions provides chairs with scaffolding on issues such as HR requirements, FERPA, faculty IT needs, marketing their programs, treasury, audit and purchasing requirements, university regulations and responsibilities, among many other bureaucratic requirements and processes.

With smart, creative staff members serving in these capacities, we have built expertise to help chairs and their departments navigate cumbersome issues. Prior to these changes, our chairs and faculty often hit dead ends, leading to frustration and annoyance in trying to achieve their goals; now our staff have such deepened understanding of how to navigate the system, they can usually find paths forward that would not be obvious otherwise. By hiring well and training well, our faculty benefit from support staff with expertise in their functional areas that outstrips what a faculty member or chair could ever know.

We have not only saved money in this model—as our staff with their deepened expertise know what questions to ask and what cost savings can be gained—we have also saved time and effort on the part of our faculty. We are able offer our faculty better support, e.g., in terms of instrumentation, marketing, travel arrangements, and technical assistance, adding value to their work.

One of the reasons the model works is the physical proximity of decanal staff. The associate deans, dean, and chief of staff all are housed in a dean's suite. The dean's office is bracketed between two offices, with an executive assistant on one side and the chief of staff on the other. This arrangement allows for information to be shared and questions answers quickly.

One risk of this model is poor communication. With such a complex operation, open communication is key. Every week the dean, associate deans, and chief of staff meet for two hours and discuss all issues pertaining to the College. The chief of staff meets biweekly with the directors/senior staff. Then, both groups (senior staff, dean, associate deans and chief of staff) meet monthly.

Another challenge is communication and expectations outside of our College. Our approach is a bit different and may not translate to other colleges at the University, we sometimes face frustration or confusion among fellow university personnel outside the College. We tend to want to move faster than our colleagues in other areas of the University and, given the higher levels of expertise, we often push for policy and procedure changes at the University level.

Another Model: Structure Based Upon Mission and Values

In a few instances, an organizational structure unlike any of the standard models has been chosen to reflect the values and mission of an institution. One such example is at The Evergreen State College, shown in this organizational chart (Figure 2.8).

Missing from this structure are department chairs or program heads. Why this structure?

From its inception, Evergreen has had an interdisciplinary curriculum. Early faculty and administrators judged that traditional structures would silo the disciplines and make it more difficult to bring them together. Additionally, the College has always had a strong egalitarian ethic, with the view that the faculty should own the curriculum, and be responsible for teaching it and its direction.

FIGURE 2.8
Model Based Upon Mission & Values

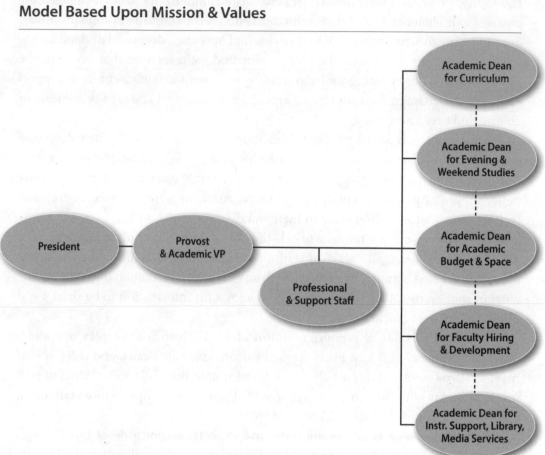

The six academic deans are appointed from the Evergreen faculty and serve as full-time administrators during their four-year renewable terms. Their roles are to:

a) provide leadership in their designated "desk assignments" or functional areas,

b) chair or serve on collegewide governance committees,

c) represent the college administration in collective bargaining with the faculty union, and

d) contribute to faculty development and evaluation.

Although the faculty are not organized by traditional disciplines and the College has no departments, the faculty opt into what are called "planning units." Planning units have conveners whose function is neither formal (i.e., represented in the organizational chart), nor does the function carry administrative appointments or receive additional compensation/release time. "No one really organizes the faculty," notes Andrew Reece, one of the academic deans. "As far as what faculty members teach, that is to some extent a negotiation between them and their colleagues and the curriculum deans."

Summary

Figure 2.9 summarizes the reporting relationships among the heads of sub-units (most often department chairs and directors of centers and of operational offices), divisional associate/assistant deans (if applicable), and the dean for each model.

FIGURE 2.9
Academic Reporting Relationships in Organizational Models[3]

I. Traditional
Chairs→ Dean

Variation: Traditional + Schools
Chairs →Dean + Chairs → School Director→Dean

II. Dean-Only
Chairs → Dean

III. VPAA/Dean of the College
Chairs and Directors → VPAA/Dean

IV. Functional + Division Deans
Type A: Functional + Portfolio Division Deans
        Chairs---›Associate Deans → Dean

Type B: Functional + Line Division Deans
        Chairs → Division Deans → Executive Dean

V. Functional + Administrative Associate/Assistant Deans & Directors
Chairs → Dean; Administrative Associate/Assistant Deans & Directors → Dean

From this review, it appears that there is a natural progression of organizational structure based upon a college's size, budget autonomy, mission (teaching-intensive vs. research-intensive) that looks something like Figure 2.10.

Ultimately, deans should plan toward an organizational model that best matches the outcomes that are important to them and their institution.

- If it's most important to you, as dean, to free up your time to focus on fund-raising, advocating for your college within and outside the University, and providing intellectual leadership to your college, you may select the Line Division Dean model because it delegates authority to associate deans.

---

[3] Some other organizational structures are not captured here. Those outside the predominant models may be a function of institutional history, collective bargaining agreements, and so forth. Fortunately most colleges post information on their websites sufficient for anyone wishing to explore these models further.

FIGURE 2.10
Evolution of College Organizations

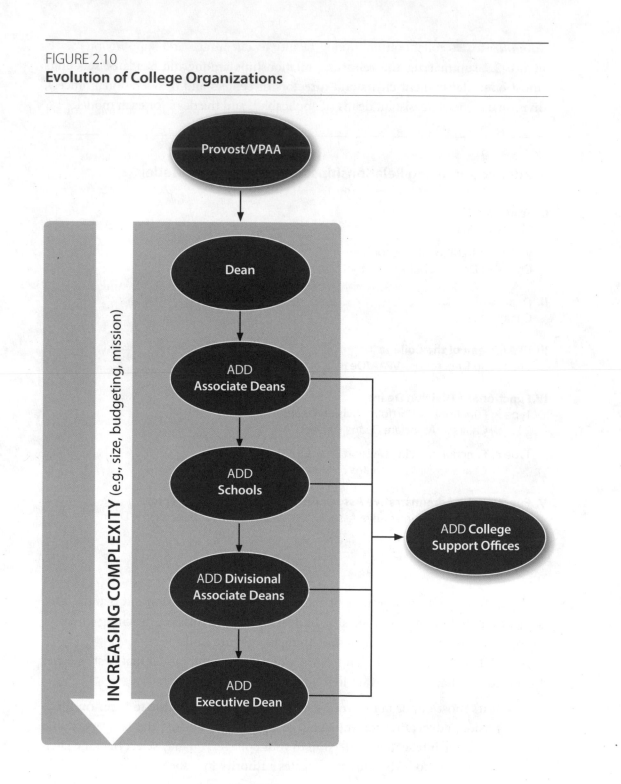

- To foster collaboration among faculty to encourage and support interdisciplinary teaching and research, you may look to either the Portfolio model or Line Division Dean models.

- To retain direct contact with your chairs and directors, the Traditional model or Portfolio Division Dean models would be appropriate choices.

- To minimize the extent to which you have to focus on operational matters, consideration of the Functional + Administrative A/A Deans & Director model would be in order.

- If decision-making among your decanal team best fits your leadership style, the Traditional model or Portfolio Division Dean models may offer the best structure.

- To maximize resources directly supporting your teaching and research missions, you may choose the Dean-Only model with its minimalist administrative levels.

- If your University or College still considers itself a liberal arts institution, retaining the model of the VPAA/Dean of the College to emphasize that liberal arts is the heart of the academic enterprise sends a strong message about your institutional mission.

Deploying Personnel in the Dean's Office

…detail orientation combined with an ability to take a
broad view; timely completion of tasks; calm under duress
(no, we are not making this up); skill at prioritizing;
innovativeness in thinking of new ways to do things combined
with a respect for old ways; a commitment to carrying through
on ideas; and, need we add, a sense of humor.
— *Job positing for an Associate Dean position*

This chapter defines the types of decanal staff—including associate and assistant deans, administrative fellows, and staff—who assist with managing and leading the dean's office. It also covers how these positions tend to be titled and how responsibilities are determined. In a variety of combinations, deans hire faculty to serve in administrative roles and professional staff to assist in supporting the responsibilities of their college. But besides occupying a place on an organizational chart and having business cards, what do the other personnel of the college do?

The extensive list of responsibilities of the dean's office spelled out in Appendix B makes it clear that an office of one single person cannot hope to manage—and lead—a college across all those efforts. It is also axiomatic that using staff members effectively and efficiently is critical to the success of the dean's office and to your longevity as dean, especially considering the cost and concerns about the over-proliferation of administrative positions.

To provide a general guide to decanal staffing, Figure 3.1 offers a model that predicts the rank and title of many decanal staff.

The two dimensions of responsibility for faculty/academic issues and of level of autonomy capture the assignments for decanal staffing. First, *the degree to which the area of responsibility is for faculty/academic issues* would be, on the high side, assignments related to research, curriculum, faculty affairs, and strategic planning. In contrast, areas of low faculty/academic responsibility include human resources, student services, and budgeting. The second dimension is the *level of autonomy of decisions,* or the degree to which decanal staff members can "speak with the voice of the dean"

FIGURE 3.1

Model Predicting Rank and Title for Decanal Staff

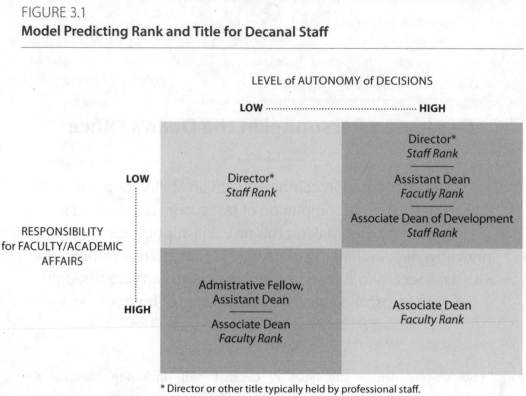

* Director or other title typically held by professional staff.

SOURCE: Websites from institutions listed in the *CCAS 2015 Membership Directory*.

without first checking with the dean.

This figure illustrates the separation between faculty administrators and professional staff administrators. Professional staff members tend to occupy areas of low faculty-related responsibilities and less autonomy, while faculty holding titles of associate dean tend to have higher responsibility for faculty/academic affairs and a greater level of autonomy. The quadrant that represents low autonomy and high faculty responsibility includes administrative fellows and some associate deans.

The quadrant represented by high autonomy with low faculty purview contains faculty assistant deans with student-related functions as well as staff associate deans assigned development responsibilities for the college. This model is a strong match with the general patterns we have found across many institutions, and thus represents a reasonable guide to decanal staff, but like anything else at universities, exceptions are relatively common.

Associate/Assistant Deans and Administrative Fellows

Faculty members serving in administrative roles in the dean's office typically carry the title of associate or assistant deans. The vast majority of colleges have at least one associate or assistant dean (abbreviated as A/AD in the rest of this chapter). Forty-five percent of CCAS member colleges have two or more associate/assistant deans. The number of A/ADs increases as pressure for the dean's office to do more increases due to everything from higher student enrollments to additional reporting requirements to leading fundraising efforts. In the broadest of terms, A/ADs are assigned to support the office either by *function* or by *division.*

Functional assistant or associate deans are assigned by function within the college—that is, they work with and represent all units of the college on certain functions such as academic affairs, research, or student services. These may be referred to as centralized, operational, or cross-college assignments. In our extensive review of college websites, where A/ADs or professional staff members are present, functional assignments are also in evidence. This holds true even at liberal arts institutions. Functional A/ADs are the most frequent type of assignment.

As an example, Table 3.1 (p 42) shows the assignments carried by functional associate deans at Oklahoma State University. One associate dean oversees instructional and personnel functions, another oversees academic programs, and a third is in charge of research and facilities.

Within those broad titles is a myriad of functional responsibilities requiring the associate dean to serve diverse constituents across the college. Note that each position's responsibilities follow logical groupings: the teaching schedule is related to faculty workload; curriculum review is linked to assessment; and supporting grant development is paired with research infrastructure and space.

Some responsibilities seem out of place, however. For example: Why are graduate student concerns given to the associate dean for academic programs? Why do graduate teaching stipends fall under the associate dean for research and facilities? Outliers are an outcome of what some call the "shoehorn effect." In other words, only so many related responsibilities can be packed into the job description of a single individual; therefore, it cannot be helped that some miscellaneous responsibilities end up in the portfolio of another A/AD or staff member.

Early in my deanship, one of my associate deans referred to his position as the "associate dean of garbage," because he was assigned all the leftover responsibilities no one else wanted or could manage. That was an indication to me that assignments among the associate deans were ready for adjustment!

—BSD

TABLE 3.1

Responsibilities of Decanal Staff in a Functional Associate Dean Model at the College of Arts & Sciences, Oklahoma State University

---

Associate Dean for Instruction and Personnel	**Associate Dean for Academic Programs**	**Associate Dean for Research and Facilities**
• Enrollment management	• Curriculum review and revisions	• Professional development for faculty in seeking and writing grants
• Academic year teaching schedule	• Program development	• Pre-award grant and contract submission process
• Summer teaching schedule	• Program assessment	• Internal grant competitions
• Professional development for department chairs	• Periodic program reviews	• Intellectual property rights
• New faculty requests	• International courses and programs	• Matching funding for grants
• Faculty searches	• Quality control for online courses and programs	• Facilitate interdisciplinary and intercollege research projects
• Administration of temporary faculty	• Interdisciplinary programs	• Grant-buyouts for faculty
• Adjunct training and support	• Academic centers for diversity	• Graduate teaching assistant stipends
• Faculty workload	• Transfer articulation agreements	• Tracking of college-level research data
• New faculty orientation	• Graduate student concerns	• Research compliance
• Management of promotion and tenure process	• Technology planning and maintenance	• Research infrastructure
• Sabbaticals	• Classroom design renovations	• Faculty start-up
• Faculty teaching support	• Other duties as assigned	• Space allocation
• Legal, policy, and procedural issues		• Facilities maintenance and planning
• Faculty grievances		• Other duties as assigned
• Academic advising and career services		
• Student retention initiatives		
• Undergraduate student issues		
• Other duties as assigned		

Functional associate deans work over the entire breadth of the college, it is unlikely they will develop a biased mindset vis-à-vis certain divisions of the college (Bright and Richards 2001, p 69). Their familiarity with the entire college makes it easier for each associate dean to understand the distinctive challenges facing departments or divisions and the office team works together to solve larger scale problems facing departments.

Division assistant or associate deans, in contrast to functional deans, represent or interact with a limited range of units. Division assignments also are referred to as substantive assignments (Krahenbuhl, 2004, p 45). Division associate deans are most likely to be found at larger comprehensive and research institutions and come in the two forms described in Chapter 2: Portfolio Division A/ADs and Line Division A/ADs.

For those Arts & Sciences colleges utilizing division A/ADs, generally two to five division deans cover the sciences, social and behavioral sciences, humanities, or arts; sometimes another is added for some version of interdisciplinary studies. The assigned divisions can be broader or more defined, with some assigned to represent two to three of these divisions (e.g., associate dean of the arts and humanities). Division assignments also occasionally appear in non-Arts and Sciences colleges, such as colleges of business (e.g., associate dean of accounting, finance and economics).

Division A/ADs are not found in isolation; in every instance, at least one functional associate dean reports to the dean as well. For example, at the University of Alaska Anchorage there are four division associate deans and a senior associate dean for academics. At the University of South Carolina, there are two division senior associate deans (one for the arts, humanities, and social sciences, the other for the sciences) along with five functional A/ADs. Using a divisional assignment structure still requires support by functionally assigned personnel.

Table 3.2 shows assignments for portfolio division associate deans (organizational Model IVA) at University of Colorado Boulder. There is one associate dean for the arts and humanities, another for the social sciences, and a third for the natural sciences. Each associate dean has 11-18 departments and academic programs reporting to them and has an additional 6-10 academic or research centers. Possessing strong liaison and management responsibilities, these associate deans manage finances, ensure all courses are covered, and provide recommendation on tenure and promotion of faculty, yet many decisions remain with the dean. There is a functional associate dean for faculty and administrative affairs. Note the associate dean for social sciences is also the dean for buildings and space, which is an example of a blended assignment model addressed later in this chapter.

In colleges where the division A/ADs make most of the decisions for the college independently of the dean, including autonomy for actions like the creation of division policies and their own hiring decisions, they would be considered line division A/ADs, as found in organizational Model IVB (and as used at The Ohio State University). No line separates portfolio from line division A/ADs; they sit at the ends of a spectrum of more dependent to less dependent upon

I have served in two different functional associate dean roles that were student focused, and in both of those roles, I worked as much or more with faculty than with students. My outlook was still broadly college focused; I did not focus on the student perspective to the extent where I no longer saw the larger strategic goals for the college.

—BSD

TABLE 3.2

Responsibilities of Decanal Staff in a Division Associate Deans Model at the College of Arts & Sciences, University of Colorado Boulder

Associate Dean for Arts and Humanities

DEPARTMENTS & PROGRAMS
- Art and Art History
- Asian Languages and Civilizations
- British Studies and Irish Studies
- Central and East European Studies
- Classics
- English
- Film Studies
- French and Italian
- Germanic and Slavic Languages & Literature
- History
- Humanities
- Jewish Studies
- Medieval and Early Modern Studies
- Philosophy
- Religious Studies
- Spanish and Portuguese
- Theatre and Dance
- Writing and Rhetoric, Program for

CENTERS
- American West, Center of the
- Anderson Language Technology Center
- Brakhage Center
- McGuire Center for International Studies
- Center for Asian Studies
- Colorado Shakespeare Festival
- CU Art Museum
- Economic Analysis, Center for
- Humanities and Arts, Center for the
- Values and Social Policy, Center for

Associate Dean for Faculty and Administrative Affairs

MAIN RESPONSIBILITIES
- A&S Faculty Council liaison
- Diversity
- Faculty recruitment
- Faculty leaves and sabbaticals
- Academic Advising
- Residential Academic Programs

PROGRAMS
- Honors Program
- Miramontes Arts and Sciences Program
- Smith Hall International Program

Associate Dean for Social Sciences, Dean for Buildings and Space*

DEPARTMENTS/PROGRAMS
- Anthropology
- Economics
- Ethnic Studies
- International Affairs
- Lesbian, Gay, Bisexual, Transgender Studies
- Linguistics
- Peace and Conflict Studies
- Political Science
- Speech, Language and Hearing Sciences
- Sociology
- Women and Gender Studies

CENTERS
- Center for the Study of Race & Ethnicity in America
- Center to Advance Research and Teaching in the Social Sciences
- Child Learning Center
- CU in D.C.
- Latin America Studies Center
- Language and Learning, Center for
- Leroy Keller Center for the Study of the First Amendment
- Service Learning
- Speech-Language & Hearing Center

Senior Associate Dean for Natural Sciences

DEPARTMENTS/PROGRAMS
- Applied Mathematics
- Astrophysical and Planetary Sciences
- Atmospheric and Oceanic Sciences
- Biology – Ecology and Evolutionary Biology
- Biology – Molecular, Cellular, & Developmental
- Chemistry and Biochemistry
- Environmental Studies
- Geography
- Geological Sciences
- Integrative Physiology
- Mathematics
- Physics
- Psychology and Neuroscience
- President's Leadership Class

CENTERS
- Center for Astrophysics and Space Astronomy
- Center for Integrated Plasma Studies
- Center for Neuroscience
- Center for Research on Training
- Energy, Minerals and Applied Research Center
- Fiske Planetarium
- Intermountain Imaging Consortium

* Includes additional responsibilities as per a functional associate dean.

the dean of the college. Both division and line associate dean assignments can work well in large colleges, freeing the dean from too many direct reports and annual evaluations, allowing them to focus on more strategic priorities including the growing demand for fundraising and working with the legislature and other external constituencies.

Using division-assigned associate deans has several benefits. Experienced senior faculty members know many of the faculty within their division, so as an associate dean, they are familiar with the people with whom they work (Bright and Richards 2001, p 69). As their research and teaching background falls within their division assignment, they also will have an invested interest in representing the division and advocating for its success. The position of division associate deans is akin to being a department head and the position can represent an easy transitional step into a future deanship.

No line separates portfolio from line division A/ADs; they sit at the ends of a spectrum of more dependent to less dependent upon the dean of the college.

One of the drawbacks of using a division associate deans model is that the college is largely managed along the lines of academic programs, which is counter to the key rationale for having a unified college of Arts and Sciences in the first place (Bright and Richards 2001, p 69). When each division is separately managed, it is too easy for division A/ADs to defend their areas beyond the point where it is productive for the college as a whole. Should antagonism develop among the divisions (and it will arise periodically), it predisposes the college to separation into discrete colleges along the divisional lines by which it is managed. The dean must regularly connect with department chairs to be aware of college progress (Bright and Richards 2001, p 69), but without circumventing the line officer function of the division associate dean (Krahenbuhl 2004, pp 45-46).

In some cases, associate deans have a "blended assignment" that includes division responsibilities as well as other functional ones. The University of Colorado Boulder acts as an example of blended associate deans (Table 3.2). The University of Notre Dame functions as another example where an associate dean is over the humanities and faculty affairs, with another associate dean heading up social sciences and research.

Blended positions come with additional challenges. First, conflicts of interest will be natural to the position. It is difficult for associate deans to make decisions truly independent of their own division, for example, when they represent the natural sciences as division A/AD as well as manage grant proposal development across the entire college in a functional role. Some deans have handled the potential for a conflict of interest by assigning the 'function' to the division A/AD with the least at stake in that function; for example, the division A/AD with few space-related challenges oversees space allocation for the college.

The second specific challenge is that any small error or oversight can be a large transgression in the eyes of others located in other academic divisions. Additionally, when a person in a blended assignment steps down or retires, the role may not be attractive to prospective candidates as both division (academic) and functional skills and knowledge are needed.

Administrative fellows are an increasingly popular method for bringing faculty expertise into the dean's office. A dean places faculty into administrative roles on a part-time or contingent basis rather than relying entirely on full-time administrators. These administrative fellows (also called faculty fellows and faculty administrative fellows) often are assigned to lead or manage a project, task force, or other specific function for the college.

Arizona State University, for instance, uses a faculty fellow to lead residential learning communities. At Oklahoma State the administrative fellow leads the college's community engagement efforts. At Virginia Tech, administrative fellows oversee specific research initiatives for the college.

Deploying administrative fellows can have powerful benefits. First, administrative fellows gain insight into how college-level administration works, which is excellent professional development for those on track for department chair or associate dean. As these positions frequently rotate, the fellows return to faculty generally as strong advocates for the function or task force they were overseeing. This practice can generate buy-in for initiatives that faculty might tend to resist (e.g., assessment of learning outcomes).

Some colleges allow administrative fellows to participate in leadership meetings for the dean's office, and faculty view such moves as improvements in shared governance. Indeed, as projects and reporting requirements in the dean's office proliferate, the dean can add additional full-time administrators, or add multiple administrative fellows with these benefits—with faculty generally favoring the latter.

A few notes of caution regarding administrative fellows: As the people appointed into these positions often have limited administrative experience, their progress on the area for which they are responsible may be lower compared to the progress a longer-service administrator might make. As with any administrative position, the effort that can be placed into the function is boundless. Assistant professors on the tenure track are poor choices for these positions because their research and/or teaching could be derailed. These appointments also require regular mentoring. Given the fresh perspective they bring to the office, others in the office seem quite happy to mentor administrative fellows.

Titles for and Background of Decanal Faculty

Our review of college websites revealed which titles are paired with which functions (Table 3.3). Most often titles are listed as "associate dean for [function]" or "assistant dean for [function]". Sometimes no additional qualifier appears in their title (their title being simply "assistant dean" or "associate dean"), making it difficult to discern their role in the office.

Clearly, no universal classification of these titles exists among Arts & Sciences decanal staff, or within other colleges at universities (checking business, education, and

TABLE 3.3
Common Associate and Assistant Dean Functional Assignments by Title*

(Faculty) Associate Dean for...	(Faculty) Assistant Dean for...	(Staff) Assistant/Associate Dean for...
Research Academic Affairs Faculty Affairs Faculty Development Diversity/Inclusion Multicultural Affairs	Enrollment Management Undergrad Research Student Affairs First year students/Retention Curriculum Assessment Class Schedules Academic Technology Academic Integrity Outreach	Finance Business Budget
Graduate Studies Undergraduate Studies Educational Affairs Curriculum Assessment Interdisciplinary Programs International Programs General Education Teaching/Instruction K-12 Education	Faculty (& Staff) Affairs† Diversity/Inclusion	Administration Human Resources Diversity/Inclusion Course schedules Student Affairs Student Success Advising
Advising Student Affairs Student Success Enrollment Management	Research†	Undergraduate Education Learning Support Outreach Admissions
Facilities Space Allocation Strategic Planning Institutional Effectiveness Community Engagement		External Relations Development/Advancement Marketing/Communications Events Alumni Affairs

*Varies depending if the individual is a faculty or staff member as shown in the different columns. Similar names have been combined (e.g. undergraduate education and undergraduate programs are represented by undergraduate studies). Boxes have been drawn around closely related functions.

† Uncommon

SOURCE: Online review of forty-nine CCAS A&S college websites conducted by authors, July 2015.

Misunderstanding how these titles are used is common. Recently, I requested changing the title of a professional staff member to assistant dean, and an HR staff member informed me those titles were reserved for faculty lines. I pointed out that a professional staff member in the college of engineering already had the title of assistant dean; the paperwork went through quickly after that.

—*BSD*

other non-A&S colleges reveals a similar jumble of who holds such positions). The number of A/ADs varies among colleges within an institution, and titles vary even among colleges comprising Arts and Sciences disciplines within the same institution. A review of CCAS member colleges with at least two assistant or associate deans reveals some 10 percent of associate deans use the title of senior with at least one of their associate dean positions, and two percent of colleges use a senior or related qualifier with at least one of their assistant dean positions. In some cases, multiple senior associate deans can be found within one college, and there can be one senior associate dean in a division assignment with the other division A/ADs not bearing the senior qualifier.

The majority of individuals holding the title of associate dean are tenured faculty members. The backgrounds of people holding the title of assistant dean are more varied. Scrutinizing the classi-fication of assistant deans at thirty-five CCAS institutions reveals that the majority (79%) of these positions is held by professional staff (71%) or non-tenure track faculty (8%). Assistant, associate, or full professors hold the title of assistant dean 21% of the time. In short, people without tenure dominate the ranks of assistant deans in CCAS colleges.

The majority of A/AD positions held by professional staff have external relations or development functions as the following ex-amples illustrate: University of Miami (Development), University of Washington (Advancement), Stanford (External Relations), and Cornell (Alumni Affairs). It makes sense to empower staff members in these positions with titles that serve to elevate the perception of their status as they are tasked with raising the profile of the institu-tion. Donors feel more privileged to work with a Senior Associate Dean of the College as compared to an Assistant Dean or even a Director of Development. Whereas titles for development staff may not have any structural meaning internal to the university, titles of perceived status are unlikely to do any harm as they aid the staff member with external constituents.

Assignment of Functions to Associate and Assistant Deans

As one may deduce from our findings on A/AD titles, associate deans who are faculty members have a variety of functional assign-ments. These assignments can be divided into distinct categories such as research, faculty affairs, academic affairs, student affairs, facilities, and planning and effectiveness (Table 3.3). Several functions from two or more categories often are combined into a single position. For instance, it is common to find associate deans for research and facilities, or an associate dean for curriculum and student affairs. Assistant deans and professional staff positions often report to associate deans, lessening the number of direct reports to the dean.

Assistant deans with faculty rank have a much narrower range of functional assignments, predominantly dealing with undergraduate programs and student affairs. Assistant deans with diversity or inclusion assignments are common, whereas assistant deans assigned to faculty-related areas are not common. Assistant deans who oversee research tend to report to an associate dean of research, a division associate dean, or are within a college where assistant deans are the predominant senior title for administrative faculty.

The number of A/AD positions held by professional staff increases with the size of the institution. Professional staff tends to oversee administration, student related functions, or development. Several of these functions—like event planning, admissions, and human resources—are distinct from faculty administrative positions. Professional staff members are more likely to be assigned financial service functions like business, finance, and budget than are faculty. This may be due to A&S faculty being untrained in financial service areas, not having an interest in these areas, or because it is more cost effective to hire staff rather than faculty for administering these functions.

Professional Staff

In addition to associate and assistant deans, deans' offices employ a diverse array of professional staff. Professional staff is defined as non-student employees (both exempt and non-exempt) who do not hold faculty rank. Professional staff assignments range from the dean's administrative assistant to financial managers to advising staff. Professional staff may report to the dean or to A/ADs.

Although titles other than associate or assistant dean typically indicate the person in the role is not in an academic appointment, this assumption is not always accurate. Many examples exist of former adjunct, part-time, or lecturer faculty who move into professional staff roles. For example, the distinction of staff positions from faculty lines blurs when advising staff members teach credit-bearing courses akin to "Introduction to the University." Likewise but uncommon, tenured faculty members sometimes transition into titles normally held by professional staff. Tenured faculty bring the "faculty side" of the college into their role and they can be an excellent fit with such administrative roles.

Professional staff is divided into two categories, exempt and non-exempt, as defined by the Fair Labor Standards Act of 1938. Exempt employees are not paid overtime; they are "exempt" from accessing overtime, meaning they work until the job is done and do not register hours. Exempt staff members often supervise other staff and/or student workers and make decisions about routine matters independent of their supervisor. Exempt staff members develop and implement policies and

New deans may be surprised at the number of staff in the dean's office categorized as exempt. I was surprised to learn that at my university all our advisor positions are classified as exempt, and all the staff supporting grant-related activity (pre- and post-award) are also exempt employees.

—BSD

procedures, with limited need for direct supervision. They often have graduate degrees, certificates, or advanced-study certificates. Exempt staff members can crudely be identified as staff checking their email outside of regular work hours and on the weekends, including at odd hours of the night. It is likely the staff members who attend a college's leadership meetings are all exempt.

Non-exempt staff must track hours and receive overtime. They are usually more closely supervised. They explain and apply policy and procedures rather than create policies. In the dean's office, these positions tend to be more 8-to-5, and these people are far less likely to be checking on their work emails during off-hours. Many professional staff members start in non-exempt positions, and then through experience, additional training, and motivation, are promoted into exempt positions.

The decision of which positions are and are not exempt is made in Human Resources. The decision is based on factors such as the responsibilities in the position description and the salary, as institutional practice (and sometimes federal policy) recommends a minimum salary threshold to be considered an exempt employee.

The distinction between these positions does matter. While universities strive to align the benefits and job security of both types of positions, the accrual of annual and sick leave is often on different schedules; exempt positions are perceived as more prestigious by their holders; and pay is usually higher. Deans want to attract and retain the best staff, and therefore position descriptions resulting in the creation of exempt positions will likely be preferred over non-exempt positions. With no time cards, exempt employees limit the amount of direct supervision required by other decanal staff.

Titles of Professional Staff and Assignment of Functions

Staff titles are far more variable than faculty titles within the dean's office. The eight titles most commonly used are manager, director, and coordinator (see Table 3.4). Many titles include a qualifier, suggesting a superior role with the qualifiers of executive or senior (e.g., executive director), or a subordinate role with the qualifiers of associate or assistant (e.g., assistant coordinator).

The functional areas assigned to staff in professional titles sort into four areas: administration; financial services and facilities; student services; and external relations. The functional areas assigned to staff are narrower than those assigned to assistant or associate deans. Positions with functional assignments such as

TABLE 3.4

Titles of Professional Staff in Deans' Offices and the Functional Areas of Their Assignments

Staff Titles*

Manager
Coordinator
Director
Officer
Chief
Specialist
Generalist
Assistant

*Some preceded with the qualifier
of Executive, Associate, Senior or
Assistant

Staff Functional Areas

Assistant to the Dean/Associate Dean
Administration
Planning
Operations
Human Resources
Affirmative Action

Finance
Business
Budget
Payroll
Accounting
Grants and Contracts
Facilities/Buildings
Information Technology

Student Services
Advising
Learning Support
Scholarships
Undergraduate Research
Student Employment
Recruitment & Retention

External Relations
Development/Advancement
Marketing/Communications
Events

NOTE: Often multiple functional areas are combined into a single staff position. The boxed functional areas represent the four main functional areas of professional staff: administration, business, student services, and external relations.

SOURCE: Online review of forty-nine CCAS A&S college websites conducted by authors in July 2015.

payroll, student employment, and affirmative action are commonplace.

Staff titles appear to be haphazard across functional areas. Looking at Table 3.4, any title in the left-hand column is likely to be found preceding any of the functional areas in the right-hand column. How administrative faculty are deployed, the history of the office, current demands, and the individual dean or associate/assistant deans present all influence how professional staff are assigned and what the positions are called.

~ ~ ~ ~ ~ ~

Our analysis of personnel reveals a tremendous variety in titles, assignment of responsibilities, and types of personnel staffing the dean's office. Our interviews with deans reveal decanal staff deployment is related to a) the number of available decanal staff positions, b) which functions are centralized outside the college or are handled within, and c) the talents, background, and interests of the people in the jobs.

Faculty members in the dean's office usually liaise directly with faculty, and professional staff members are found in functional positions that support faculty and students. Yet there are enough exceptions to conclude that deans possess flexibility in structuring the responsibilities of their offices. There is no "one right way" to organize decanal staff. Deans appear to have the freedom to deploy their team to best fit the needs of their college.

After exploring how colleges and office staff can be organized in Chapters 2 and 3, the reader might be itching to try something new. Caution is recommended. People and policies need to be consulted, and there are many options. The next chapter offers a framework for determining if your college might benefit from reorganization.

Assessing the Potential for Change

If you do not change direction,
you may end up where you are heading.

—*Lao Tzu*

A s dean, you may possess an intuitive sense that your college needs a change in structure, or that your college needs a change in procedures. This chapter suggests methods for assessing the need for re-organization within your college. This "environmental scan" covers work assignments within the dean's office, policies and practices in place, policies and procedures not in place, and how quickly a change might take place.

Deans are free to make decisions about how to organize at least some aspects of their college's administration. Of course, you have to live with the consequences of your choices. And faculty are usually quick to point out they can outlast any decision made by any administrator. After working through this chapter, you should have a qualitative data framework for making a more informed decision about the need for organizational change. You need to consider if the college is poised for an organizational change, or if an alternative to reorganize might better address the challenges facing the college.

Testing Your Assumptions About the Need for Change

As you begin to explore changing aspects of the dean's office, you should examine certain assumptions you may hold to ensure you are considering change for the right reasons.

For example, problems with administration in a college may be an artifact of the people working in the office, in which case staffing changes–although potentially painful–would be in order. Your office has support staff and often support faculty serving in the roles of associate or assistant deans, but do you have the right people working in the office? Or, as Collins (2001) phrases it: Do you have the right people on the bus?

A survey to department heads, faculty and staff can be revealing about how the dean's office staff members interact with units. Such surveys should be regularly conducted. We all have people with whom we enjoy working and there are always people whose mere presence in a room drops the temperature to below freezing, but a survey can provide other details about performance of the dean's office. In talking to colleagues, we found it surprising how few deans survey their units on a regular basis.

Likewise, you might assume meetings and communication in the college functions as well as it can in the current structure, and it is the structure itself that needs to change. Are you sure this assumption is accurate? As anyone who has served on external review teams for departments, colleges, or universities will admit, "communication problems" are always one of the top three difficulties identified by university stakeholders.

The breadth of responsibilities in the dean's office is dizzying.

Having fellow deans or external colleagues review how your office operates will reveal improvements that can be made without changing structure. The question you can then ask is: Will those improvements be sufficient to overcome the identified problems that must change?

If a different office organization would require additional resources (e.g., a divisional structure often requires the addition of one additional associate dean and a support staff member), how would your office function if you added these people to the existing structure and simply changed the division of labor in the office? Changing structure takes a great deal of time and effort. Hiring an additional staff member and rearranging personnel responsibilities is quite simple by comparison and may solve your identified problems.

If the purpose of reorganization is to identify a model requiring fewer resources (e.g., in response to budget cuts or to demonstrate financial prudence), what goals need to be met? Are you looking for the most painless way to accomplish this change (e.g., get past this while minimizing political repercussions)? Do you need the fastest way to do this (e.g., meet a deadline set by a superior)? Are you interested in how you can take advantage of the reorganization to improve services to students, faculty and other stakeholders simultaneously? Unequivocally, if time and politics allow, the latter perspective is the best approach.

Assessing the Responsibilities of Dean's Office Staff

As mentioned in earlier chapters, academic and staff members in the dean's office provide support for a wide array of activities. In fact, the breadth of responsibilities in the dean's office is dizzying. In conversation with deans at Oklahoma State University and with deans of Arts and Sciences on the Board of Directors of CCAS, we developed a comprehensive suite of responsibilities often found in dean's offices (see Appendix B). While not every activity will be done in every college (e.g., many professional graduate colleges are unlikely to be concerned with general education) or on every campus (e.g., some campuses do not conduct animal research so would not need an Institutional Animal Care and Use Committee), your office may be responsible for more than you realized.

Fortunately, responsibilities often are shared with other support offices on campus. For example, most institutions undergo a periodic review of their academic programs and although your office may be responsible for providing data and logistical support for the review, faculty in their respective departments most likely conduct the review, with the provost's office or the president's office tracking and informing your office on schedules necessary for the review. Some of the listed responsibilities are found under several subheadings, such as ADA compliance, which is under administration (e.g., training department heads, monitoring compliance, and managing complaints) as well as under academic programs and instruction (e.g., how to modify classrooms, laboratories, and websites for accessibility).

Knowing that most responsibilities are shared with other offices— and that the effort needed to attend to these responsibilities varies— it is important to assess the responsibility and effort of your college in these different functional areas.

The time needed to address all these responsibilities varies by institution and by college. Colleges of Arts and Sciences may need to commit large amounts of time and effort to general education oversight, whereas a College of Human Sciences will need less. Colleges in a large university may spend much more time with articulation agreements with community colleges than would be necessary at a private liberal arts college, which translates into a corresponding difference in effort at the level of the dean's office.

Knowing that most responsibilities are shared with other offices—and that the effort needed to attend to these responsibilities varies—it is important to assess the responsibility and effort of your college in these different functional areas. We suggest a beneficial exercise is for you and your staff to use Appendix B to personalize these responsibilities and efforts to your situation. For the first step of this exercise, the graphic rating scale under the right columns in Appendix B can be used to assess 1) the degree to which you are responsible for an activity (Locus of Responsibility), and 2) the relative amount of time and effort your office commits to that activity on an annual basis (Effort and/or Time Commitment).

We recommend you copy these pages from the book and have each staff member in your office complete this activity based on their assigned responsibilities and other activities with which they are involved even if not part of their assigned duties. Answers should be from the perspective of current responsibilities within the dean's office. For instance, the role of program faculty in assessing student-learning outcomes may be paramount to the tangential role played by staff members in the dean's office, leading your staff to notate its more limited effort and time commitment.

The second step of this exercise identifies gaps in responsibilities. Go through Appendix B again and note where your team feels the responsibility is not being addressed at all or addressed poorly. Of these marked activities, highlight the ones that should be addressed or improved and that your college has the ability to act upon. For example, if the university does not offer a structured program for onboarding new department heads, that is an activity for which your office could be responsible. If no one on your staff is putting much thought effort into this, you have uncovered an opportunity to add an important service for the college.

You should make a note of these responsibility gaps. But be careful not to list responsibility gaps unnecessarily; many of these services may be centralized at the university. If you have a legal office that takes care of all referrals and it works smoothly this way, this is not an activity you should add to your office. You may find other instances where several people contribute to a common responsibility. Keep in mind that it is possible this is redundant or confusing for department heads and faculty to know which person to consult on that issue and may represent an operational inefficiency.

Assessing the College's "Standards of Practice"

How can the data collected so far be used? Before drawing firm conclusions based on this information alone, consider reviewing your operations through the *CCAS Standards of Practice* (2013). These standards were developed and tested by the CCAS Board of Directors to provide a self-assessment instrument to explore the policies and procedures in place within a college. The intent of the Standards is to allow deans and members of their staff to evaluate their policies and procedures relative to best practices in colleges across the nation. The *Standards of Practice* has been widely presented at CCAS and other professional meetings, and many deans have used it as a self-assessment instrument to review their compliance with these practices. The document can be accessed at the CCAS website, *www.ccas.net*, under Resources > Standards of Practice.

The intent of the Standards is to allow deans and members of their staff to evaluate their policies and procedures relative to best practices in colleges across the nation.

While the online document allows you to consider the presence or absence of policies, the associated scoring rubric is quite helpful in better understanding the use of the policies and practices in a college. This Excel-based scoring rubric is available to CCAS members from the *www.ccas.net* homepage under Resources > Standards of Practice > Standards of Practice Scoring Rubric. Non-members of CCAS can reconstruct the rubric scores from a paper-based exercise. To conduct the self-assessment, provide e-copies of the rubric or copy the pages from the publication to each staff member in your office to complete this activity independently based upon their working knowledge of the college's policies and practices.

The scoring is a 1, 2, 3, or NA for each policy as follows:

1 = Question can be answered in the affirmative without equivocation. Policy/practice is well understood and regularly adhered to.

2 = Partially true. May be a formal policy but is not uniformly adhered to. May be a standard practice but is not codified. Parties within the College may have different answers to the question.

3 = Policy/practice is virtually absent, sporadic, non-uniform, and not well understood.

N/A = Not applicable. This rating should be used sparingly.

After gathering the feedback, look at what you collect from each individual first. You might observe several instances where one or more people marked a 3 and there also might be a single moment where one person marked a 1. These answers tell you a policy or practice is in place and is followed by someone, but others are completely unaware.

Discrepancies in your office could be due to the compartmentalized nature of some of the positions in the dean's office or there is limited internal communication on the availability of the policies that results in this pattern. If you make the logical extension of finding 3's paired with 1's, faculty, staff, and unit administrators may also be unaware of the policies already in place, and it would behoove your office to better communicate with the college's employees.

The second step in this self-assessment is to talk through the scores with all the participants around a table and discuss how the varied scores should be combined into a single number for that policy. It is not just an average of the scores received; you are trying to understand if the policy or practice exists, and to what extent the lack of knowledge of its existence/use is due to the narrowness of its use which could still be scored a 1 or if in fact the policy should be known or applied better than it actually is which should be scored a 2.

An example of how a policy may be in place but unfamiliar to many comes from Bret's office in the response to the standard, "Are there procedures for establishing, reviewing, and eliminating centers, institutes, and similar interdisciplinary entities?" When his staff conducted the self-assessment, there was a comprehensive policy in place and was followed, but it was only known by people in centers or already in contact with the dean's office about proposing one. Although other staff members in the office not associated with centers were unaware of the policy, this score was kept as a 1 and it was noted that communication about its existence should be improved. There will be some items or areas where everyone scores the policy a 3 and multiple scores of missing policies in the same area will reveal a deficit of attention by your office.

You should make note of the areas that score lower than other areas and use those as part of assessing your office in the next section of this chapter. When the staff in Bret's office completed the exercise, almost every policy or practice relating to non-tenure track faculty was found to be absent in the College and subsequently scored as a 3 by everyone. This revelation helped pinpoint an area that needed to be addressed.

Using the Assessment Data

With the internal survey of office responsibilities and assessment of policies and practices in hand, you have insight into the strengths and weaknesses of your office's current organization. Your strengths are identified by the 1's on the *Standards of Practice* survey. You probably see sections in which your college does well. Similarly, you might have a high level of responsibility in many functional areas from Appendix B and have people spending a lot of their effort on those areas. You should also have areas of strength in service identified through the survey of department chairs, faculty, and staff mentioned earlier in this chapter.

[Weaknesses] come in three common forms: lack of appropriate policy or procedures, insufficient effort in some (or many) areas of responsibility, and inadequate adherence to policy or procedures.

Congratulations! Deans don't often have time to think about the positive aspects of their administration. Hold onto this moment for as long as you can!

Then consider the weaknesses you uncovered. These come in three common forms: lack of appropriate policy or procedures, insufficient effort in some (or many) areas of responsibility, and inadequate adherence to policy or procedures.

The *lack of policy or procedures* (3's on the *Standards of Practice* combined scores) should be relatively straightforward to resolve. Prioritizing the development of policies, working through several of them each semester with a college shared-governance committee until they have been created could be a 3-year to 4-year process, but is not overly complex. Once new policies are in place, however, unless someone makes others aware of them and supports their implementation, you will only change your *Standards of Practice* score to a 2 as the policy may not be well know or followed.

The other two forms of weaknesses are most often due to insufficient staffing in the dean's office. *Insufficient effort* is where you identified responsibilities in your office that are underserved by staff time. *Inadequate adherence to policy* is generally seen as 2's on the combined scores of your *Standards of Practice*. The earlier example from Bret's office was with respect to non-tenure track faculty, and leading and managing international programs was another found in his office. Such gaps might result from a shortage of staff time as there is only so much effort than can be crammed into a work week.

If you need to add effort onto some activities, you can reassign someone's time allocation to that effort, but of course it stands to reason that they will have to do other activities with less time and effort. You may be able to create some efficiencies in effort, creating space for additional duties. People working across categories (e.g., working in research, faculty affairs, and curriculum) are unlikely to work as efficiently as those who work within categories (e.g., focus only on supporting research).

Further, you may be able to create efficiencies across the college by centralizing services. For example, Bret is considering centralizing all travel services for his college. As software used for this is cumbersome and frequently changing, having a few people in the dean's office with that responsibility should reduce the total staffing needs in departments.

The most likely way to add effort, however, is to add positions. As people are added to the dean's office, how they are deployed is a primary driver in shifting among organizational models (see Figure 2.10 in Chapter 2). Which people to add to your office (e.g., exempt or non-exempt staff, divisional associate deans) requires careful consideration as a general goal should be to maximize efficiency while minimizing financial and political costs.

How Quickly is Change Needed?

The above assessments can provide insight into the need for changing where or how much effort is used in the dean's office. Using your intuitive sense that change may be needed, you now are aware of other factors that have come into play through your environmental scan.

For example, perhaps you cannot finish all the assigned reports expected from your office. Or maybe no one in your office possesses anything resembling a work-life balance. Perhaps the position of department chair in your college has a huge rate of turnover and faculty are reluctant to step into open chair positions. Change may be needed more quickly in some cases than in others.

Change invariably involves resources. Some resources may be "one-time use," such as an investment of time to develop a new policy or purchasing new software and training the office staff in its use. Other costs are ongoing in nature as with a new person and the associated office and ongoing professional development expenses. To explore if the timing might be right for a change of organization or staffing in your office given the university context, it is helpful to explore the following questions. You are trying to construct an answer to the invariably asked question of "why now?"

- Will the proposed change in organizational structure actually help address the office's current shortcomings you identified through the exercises in this chapter?

- Do the needed changes in services align with either the university or college strategic plan?

- Will the financial investment be neutral due to reallocation of effort or reassignment of responsibilities?

- If additional resources are required, will you receive support from your superiors and reports that this is an acceptable place to invest these resources given other needs within the college?

- Would a change itself be supported by your superiors, and will your superiors be around long enough to support the change through to its completion?

- Would the change itself be supported or at least be understood by department heads and faculty?

- Are there other change actions underway in the office that would be negatively, or positively, impacted by such a change?

- Do your office staff expect this change will still be needed in the college five or more years from now?

A Framework for Optimizing Successful Change

From our interviews and discussions with deans who have considered, implemented, or have been subject to a change in their college's organizational structure, it is clear deans often have an intuitive sense of what actions and processes can help make a change process successful. Many of those whom we interviewed mention such things as: "I kept my provost informed;" "Faculty have to be part of the process from the beginning;" and "Our university has policies that tell us what steps we needed to follow."

Such comments fall within a framework for organizational change first proposed by Lee Bolman and Terry Deal in their landmark book, *Modern Approaches to Understanding and Managing Organizations* (1984) and further refined and applied in numerous subsequent publications. In fact, in his 2014 book *Change Leadership in Higher Education*, Jeffery L. Buller calls their framework "perhaps the most familiar way" used to describe the process of reexamining change and organizational culture in higher education (p 39).

This model suggests there are four "frames" at play in organizational dynamics: Structural, Political, Human Resource, and Symbolic. We propose that deans use this framework as a backdrop as they are considering changes to their college (either their office model or at the departmental level). Being attentive to and reflective about each of these frames as you initiate and process changes—while not guaranteeing success—can at the least ensure that you are not missing any landmines.

TABLE 4.1
Frames and Central Concepts in an Organization

Structural	**Political**	**Human Resource**	**Symbolic**
Rules	Power	Needs	Culture
Roles	Conflict	Skills	Meaning
Goals	Competition	Relationships	Metaphor
Policies	Organizational politics		Ritual
Technology			Ceremony
Environmnet			Stories
			Heroes

SOURCE: Bolman and Deal, *Modern Approaches to Understanding and Managing Organizations,* 1984.

For purposes of considering college organization issues, the application of each frame would be:

Structural

Deans sit within a larger organizational context. The Structural frame encompasses the rules, policies, procedures, roles, and assignments that set contexts and boundaries for how a dean can act.

Political

Any environment includes dynamics of influence, power, and relationships. Situations need to be examined keeping in mind the motivations, alliances, differences, conflict, and sources of support (from above and below) for your actions as a dean.

Human Resource

You get the most out of people when they feel valued, heard, fully utilized for their talents and skills, and when they are offered opportunities to grow. The Human Resource frame attends to how people feel and what needs they seek to have satisfied.

Symbolic

"We're all in this together." Symbolic gestures and events acknowledge the need to give larger meaning to change events through celebrations, recognitions, and reminding people in your college that they are part of a shared vision or purpose.

Table 4.2 enumerates under each frame the kinds of questions a dean might ask him/herself as they contemplate, prepare for, and implement change.

TABLE 4.2
Questions Through the Four Frames

STRUCTURAL

- In what situations do I have the authority to make independent decisions and when are my decisions dependent upon others?
- Do the proposed changes actually address the causes of the identified problem?
- Have you assessed financial implications of your proposed change, both short and long term?
- Are you following relevant policies and procedures in the college/university/ system for making the changes?
- If the change you are considering involves moving faculty lines or changing job descriptions, what are the pertinent policies and contracts?
- Have you considered space allocation and prioritizing continuous space in your decision (e.g., proximity of programs falling under one department chair, where will a new center or service office be located)?

POLITICAL

- Have you identified the nature or reason for the existing conflict in units in order to craft appropriate solutions?
- Have you brought the right people together to collaboratively develop a change that fits the identified challenges?
- Do you regularly brainstorm options with a trusted group who you can rely on for candid, insightful feedback?
- Have you clarified the need for change with constituents and received feedback?
- Is your proposed change backed by data to buttress your arguments (e.g., peer comparisons, financial ramifications)?
- Is your rationale for change overly based on your own avoidance of conflict (e.g., allow a nettlesome department to move to another college just so you don't have to manage it)?
- Have you taken the time to assess the power dynamic in the college?
- Have you vetted your proposed changes up and down the line?
- Have you appropriately involved the provost along the way?
- Have you ensured sufficient buy-in among key faculty leaders and committees in the college?
- Have you achieved sufficient understanding by key external stakeholders (e.g., influential alumni/friends of the college) so that they do not become advocates against change with the provost, president, or the university's governing board?
- Have you advertised your change in the context of the larger vision for the college or its impact?
- Are any institutional dynamics at play that will affect the chances of your proposed change being accepted (frequent turnover in the dean's position; pressure from the president to grow enrollments)?
- If an externally imposed change is planned, are you aware how your actions and reactions will be perceived by the provost and other constituencies?
- What are your plans to continue to encourage harmony after the change has been implemented?

HUMAN RESOURCE

- Are you attentive to how reorganization in the dean's office represents interests in each department (e.g., clustering of responsibilities, degree area of the individual being hired)?
- Are you attentive to how your decision will be viewed by tenured/ tenure-track faculty?
- Have stakeholders been regularly updated on assessment of the problems and decisions along the way?
- How do you communicate about the change so individuals do not take it personally?
- Have you used a variety of media to communicate the change (e.g., 1-on-1 meetings, emails, newsletters, town halls, social gatherings)?
- How well matched are people with the expectations and descriptions of their positions?
- Can you move people among positions to reduce conflict?
- As personnel come and go, are you attending to the different skill sets that people bring to the position?
- Prior to changing a job description or shifting the responsibility for a task, have you holistically reviewed the responsibilities of all support staff to optimize bundling of responsibilities?
- If the change involves changes in roles and /or responsibilities of people, what will the impact be on individuals? Does it offer something positive for that change (e.g., salary increase, title change, professional growth) or potentially negative (elimination of position, taking on extra duties, reporting to someone different who they don't like as well)?
- Does your office model provide potential growth opportunities in administration for faculty and staff?
- Have you considered cross-training support staff in key office responsibilities?
- Are the desks or offices of support personnel with similar functions or responsibilities proximate to each other?
- What mechanisms might you employ to alleviate faculty and staff concerns about change (e.g., joint appointments, callback options)?

SYMBOLIC

- Have you done an advertised listening tour of key constituents?
- Are you considering the potential to provide symbolic meaning for the change (e.g., elevate the status of the arts, show your shared pain in budget cuts, sense of equity)?
- Can you time the change with another meaningful event (e.g., anniversary of the university or college, key retirement, budget cuts)?
- Have you fully utilized publicity vehicles to shed a positive light on the change?
- How will you celebrate or otherwise demonstrate the change has occurred?

~ ~ ~ ~ ~ ~

This chapter helps set the stage for change by suggesting you conduct an environmental scan of the functioning of your office and begin considering the factors that need to be attended to for change to be successful. You now have some qualitative data that identifies areas for improvement in your office, and you thought through the timing of change as it applies to the organizational structure of your office. This information will help you articulate the justifications for and against reorganization with your superiors, peers, and those whom you represent.

The next two chapters explore the change process itself—to assist you in building the case not just for why change may be beneficial, but for how to work through the process in a constructive manner.

Implementing Organizational Change
Within the Dean's Office

*Find a way for people to get the job done while
feeling good about what they are doing.*
—*Bolman and Deal (2003)*

Deans may feel they possess little control over the many transactions flowing
through their office. A dean cannot prioritize every decision or task—from
travel and purchasing approvals, to personnel actions, to the daily calendar—so they must focus their efforts selectively. Deans do, however, exercise control
over the organization of their office staff. Decisions about how many people work in
the office, their titles, their responsibilities, and who occupies the positions rest largely
in the hands of the dean.

Evaluating the effectiveness of your office should not be a one-and-done event
because the performance of your staff is central to supporting your faculty, programs,
and students. If you find the operation falling short, some changes may be in order.
This chapter addresses reorganizing the dean's office to try to match structure with
the functions of the office. Examples of changes are included, with brackets indicating
how the change process illustrates one of the Four Frames in an Organization (see
Chapter 4).

Adding Positions

Adding new positions is one of the most problematic changes that can be made in the
dean's office. Regardless of their veracity, accounts in the media point to ballooning
administrative positions as compared to faculty lines and how administrative costs
are driving up the cost of attending college. In short, adding new positions will be
scrutinized.

A few things should be kept in mind when considering the number of positions in
your office. If you come in as a new dean to a situation where adding new positions
has been endorsed by the provost, do not assume everyone will be supportive. Adding

new positions may be interpreted as evidence about how you handle challenges—you solve your own problems first, and then look to helping others. Although it is unlikely you want to be viewed in this manner, faculty will gladly interpret your actions for you. Therefore, take time to learn about the college and its needs. If adding a staff member is appropriate, take the time to obtain buy-in from the provost, department heads, and faculty.

Adding a person to your office means, of course, there will be a new reporting line, as that person needs to report to someone. One dean reported to us that his current situation of having thirty direct reports strains his capacity to supervise all of these individuals effectively. Therefore, if he creates a new position, someone other than him would need to be the supervisor.

Examples abound about how deans have used creative approaches to solve staffing issues in their offices.

Adding a person also impacts the responsibilities of someone else in the office. For example, if you create a position for an IT manager, someone in the office was performing pieces of that job. When the new person comes on board and the other individual is relieved from it, be assured that the remaining responsibilities of the person relieved of the task will expand to fill the workload space just created.

Covering new responsibilities by adding positions can be a driver of "administrative bloat." All deans want their offices to perform every task to the highest standard, but in resource-limited systems, not enough staff can be hired to reach such a standard. A perpetual struggle in the dean's office is deciding what aspects of the office work are getting done "good enough"—not poorly where faculty or students are suffering as a result—but not done so well that spending these resources is at the expense of other areas in the college or its units.

Therefore, you need to decide the following when hiring a new person: Do you want existing personnel to focus more time and quality effort on their existing responsibilities (default), or do you want them to take on a new responsibility? If it is a new responsibility, communicate this to them well in advance of the hiring of the new staff member for them to begin envisioning how they might factor the new responsibility into their workload.

Examples abound about how deans have used creative approaches to solve staffing issues in their offices. When a new dean at a public master's university walked into her job, it became clear her predecessor had relied on a model of minimizing the activities run through the dean's office. With no time available to the dean for fundraising, and with the provost's office in the process of moving more responsibilities down to the dean's office, she realized there was insufficient staff in the office for all the work needing to be done. Her options were limited, however, as the upper administration at her university—wary of increasing the number of administrative positions—had placed a cap on the number of faculty serving as associate/assistant deans

[Structural]. The office was already at the limit.

The dean believed she needed an individual to support faculty engaged in external grant applications. She made a case to her college's leadership council to add a grants officer (a staff position) and involved her provost in the discussion [Political]. She stressed the imperative for increasing grants coming to the college to buttress her case for why resources should be put into such a development position, and the leadership council and provost supported the change.

Cognizant of the limit on associate/assistant deans, but seeing more opportunities for faculty-level involvement, she created three administrative fellow positions (faculty re-assigned part time to the dean's office): one to oversee assessment, another to oversee centers, and a third to run the faculty mentor program. These administrative fellows became part of a "future leaders" program in the college, providing opportunities for faculty to experience administration while knowing they will rotate back into their normal faculty lines when desired.

Once these faculty and staff were working in the office and started "digging into" the work to be done, only then did the enormity of the tasks they were assigned become apparent, leading to the obvious conclusion: additional support staff was needed. This example illustrates well how internal reorganization is an ongoing endeavor rather than a one-time activity.

Shifting Staff Responsibilities

A new dean at a public research university took a similar approach to adding part-time faculty lines to the office without adding full-time administrative positions. The dean created a suite of faculty-support members who, as part of the dean's leadership team, each assumed well-defined responsibilities: equal opportunity liaison; coordinator of international programs; interdisciplinary program development; women in science; scholarship coordinator. The dean appoints individuals she believes are well suited to the needs of the position (and the potential to be future administrators) to two-year positions without a search, and provides a teaching load reduction or a summer salary. This approach is another example of creatively increasing staffing in the office without adding new positions, as well as supporting the professional development of faculty [Human Resource].

A dean at another public research university was in the unfortunate circumstance of needing to let a staff member go due to reductions in budget. He discussed this pending dismissal with the provost, who recognized the difficulty of the situation but understood the need to eliminate the position [Human Resource]. Later, when the staff member to be released showed up at the provost's office to complain, the provost knew about the situation [Political], allowing the dean to proceed as planned.

Have you ever found yourself hoping a staff member in your office would retire to allow you to revise the position description to better match the needs of the office? If so, you are probably in the camp of administrators not wishing to confront conflict directly. The responsibilities of every position in the office changes through time, and if you don't lead the charge to keep the office responsive to current needs, the faculty of the college and even the office staff will be awaiting your retirement!

For example, not long ago, deans were not heavily involved in fundraising—but these days it often represents a quarter of a dean's workload. Similarly, student advisement used to be little more than assuring students had planned a reasonable course schedule for their next semester. With an increasing focus on student success, advising now encompasses the entire student experience—from early alert grade discussions, to study skills, identifying support networks, and career advice—along with course scheduling. As higher education continues to evolve, so must the responsibilities of the dean's office staff.

The earlier in the process you can update the provost on your analysis of the need for change the better; the provost will be more apt to view these changes as a positive sign of your leadership.

Adjusting the responsibilities of office staff is both necessary and anticipated, and therefore it is usually the simplest change you can make in the office. Of course such changes should be discussed within your office and with Human Resources where appropriate if it impacts staff job descriptions, for instance. But the need to discuss changes with the provost or units of the college depends on the scale of the change. You need a staff member to stop filing paper records and start maintaining an electronic database? Don't check with the provost; this one is on you. Do you want to place oversight of advisement and curriculum under the same associate dean, necessitating a change in who participates on a university committee? You want to check in with your boss for something like that.

The way you inform the provost is important. If you think you should make the change but want advice, ask the provost for an opinion. Realize if the provost recommends against the proposal and you decide to do it anyway, this decision may put you in the uncomfortable position of either holding back the potential of your office or getting on the wrong side of the provost.

If you must make the change, outlining the rationale for the reorganization is as much as you should do. In this case, you are not asking permission to make the change; rather you are making the provost aware of the reorganization and how it will benefit the college, and ultimately the university. Further, the earlier in the process you can update the provost on your analysis of the need for change the better; the provost will be more apt to view these changes as a positive sign of your leadership.

Since the responsibilities of positions shift on a regular basis to keep up with the changing office needs, reassignments can be done through a thoughtful conversation with the individuals, followed by a memo outlining the changed duties. When the reorganization runs deeper, or is driven by budgetary changes, the process can be more complex. What follows are examples of how some other deans approached realignment of responsibilities.

When starting in her role, a dean at a public research university observed how the associate deans and staff in the office interacted and performed their duties. She soon recognized that the position responsibilities—and maybe even the people in those positions—needed to change. As she developed an organizational chart with job descriptions and reporting lines in anticipation of reorganizing, she did not put people's names in the boxes on the organizational chart, as she did not want to create a job for a particular person. Instead, she wanted the ideal organization for the college [Structural].

Because there are real people in the current positions with whom she would like to maintain relationships, she wanted to move thoughtfully and slowly [Human Resource]. When she realized some staff members serving "at will" would need to be replaced as they no longer fit the new position descriptions, she received the backing of the provost before proceeding further [Political]. Instead of running the searches herself, she asked an associate dean of a different college to chair each of the searches. This helped the reorganization process to appear as the best choice for the college and university, and not just for the dean [Political]. Further, this approach distanced her from the frustrations of individuals who supported the occupants of each position, which might have otherwise resulted in disrupting the search process or weakening the support for the new staff chosen for those positions [Human Resource].

In another case, an associate dean at a private research university was tasked by the dean with reorganizing the roles of staff positions in the office due to budget reductions. The associate dean went to Human Resources to initiate this discussion and found an HR person skilled in running reorganization processes. The HR representative kept the associate dean (and thus, the dean) aware of each step of the process, including how to group activities into categories and how to align categories of tasks [Structural] (similar to the activity described in Chapter 3 and Appendix B). This structural approach allowed the dean's office to envision how the office could function with fewer staff members and to reconfigure the physical layout of the dean's office to align the work areas of the staff with their revised responsibilities.

A dean may not consider changing to whom a person reports as changing their responsibilities, but this change can be perceived as such by staff. For example, upon arriving at a large public research university, a new dean learned the director of the college's communication efforts was supervised by one of the associate deans. Unfortunately, the two had a combative relationship. Until he could understand how to repair their relationship (or determine if one of them needed to be replaced), he shifted the reporting line of the director of communications to himself. Later, when an assistant dean was replaced with a faculty member skilled in external communications, he moved the reporting line of the director to her.

This change may sound simple enough, but it was not. From the communication director's perspective, when she began reporting to the dean, she also had to start working closely with the foundation staff on fundraising efforts, which was a new responsibility. Similarly, when reassigned to the assistant dean, she was expected to support the marketing of online and travel courses. Although her responsibilities never changed on paper, each supervisor had a different expectation of what those responsibilities meant. With each new supervisor, the assumed responsibilities of the director grew. Just like reassigning specific responsibilities, moving a reporting line should be approached with the expectation that responsibilities also will change.

Except for internal office concerns, reassigning the reporting lines of staff seems to incur little political risk to the dean. A few deans reported that some faculty members were agitated because they used to work with a specific person and they did not want this to change. But a brief visit from the dean who acknowledged their frustration—coupled with a) an explanation of how the adjustment could improve dean's office services to them overall and b) a statement of appreciation for their support of this change as it was for the greater good of all faculty and/or students in the college—mitigated their concerns.

If you have not already drawn the following conclusion, remember—the final line of job descriptions for any staff member in the dean's office should always read *"and other responsibilities as assigned by the dean."*

Changing Titles

Despite the complexity of titles used in the academy (see Chapter 3), they do provide some insight into the person's responsibilities in the office. The phrase "some insight" is used as position descriptions often include 15+ responsibilities, of which the top one to three should be captured in the title.

Staff

The titles of non-faculty positions often are controlled by the institution's Human Resource office, which maintains a list of general responsibilities for specific titles. Much to the vexation of deans, the allowable salary range is often specified. You might be familiar with situations where department heads and directors attempt to modify position descriptions just so the dean can apply for a change in title for the staff member, which—oh yes—is associated with a pay increase for the staff member.

For the most part, staff members are not concerned about their titles, except for how they relate to promotion and salary, and for some, how a title ranks them in terms of seniority. A conversation with the staff member and the supervisor (if it isn't you) is often enough to determine if there is interest in a title change and the potential for change in responsibilities and benefits. If there is an associated salary change, getting agreement with the provost in advance of the name change is advisable.

One aspect of a title must be attended to: whether it confers 'non-exempt' or 'exempt' status on the employee. This difference legally implies a distinct suite of responsibilities and benefits associated with the position, so deans should bear this in mind when selecting titles.

One dean faced a dilemma concerning a staff member who held the title of director, had an Ed.D., and led a large student services office for the college. The job entailed oversight of student recruitment, advising, career services, scholarships, and several retention, progression, and graduation initiatives. She was not considered as having an equal voice by some departments, however, which they manifested by ignoring or resisting her recommendations for improvement.

The dean believed the title of assistant dean was more appropriate for her scope of responsibility and would signal that she was a full member of the dean's leadership team and deserved a concomitant level of respect [Symbolic]. Because this title had only been held by faculty, he elected to run the concept of the title change by the college's faculty council [Structural, Political]. The faculty recommended overwhelmingly that the title change be approved, and once the change had been effectuated, the departments opposing her became more open to hearing her ideas for improvement.

New deans—and those trying to keep the office operations current with changes in higher education—might want to be involved in areas critical for the improvement of the college.

Faculty

The process of title change for a faculty member tends to be less complicated than for staff. However, as Roper and Deal (2010) state, the symbolic frame is the most overlooked, which has implications for naming faculty positions in the dean's office.

For most institutions, the position of associate dean outranks assistant dean, and the prefix of senior or executive indicates an administrative rank above those without the prefix. The trailing words are more important for external recognition of the position, as they signify the general description of the position (which, as for staff, at least hit the highlights of their responsibilities) and identify the priorities of the dean's office. However, there are few immediate stakeholders in the choice of these titles except for the dean and the specific individuals in the position. Yet such titles hold significant symbolic power, indicating the priorities you have identified for the dean's office.

New deans—and those trying to keep the office operations current with changes in higher education—might want to be involved in areas critical for the improvement of the college. As dean, if you oversee program assessment, it does not make sense for an associate dean to have the word "assessment" in their title.

Similarly, it may be important symbolically to include a specific word or phrase in an associate/assistant dean's title, demonstrating someone is responsible for this activity in the dean's office. One example would be "Diversity" or "Inclusive Excellence." These titles are appearing more frequently in administrative titles. Of late, many colleges are adding "Community Engagement" to administrative faculty titles, internally and externally signifying the importance of such activities for their college [Political, Symbolic].

Again, except for the need to keep him or her in the loop, there is rarely reason to discuss or ask permission from the provost. Since a title change does not indicate a change in salary or exemption status for faculty, the change process tends to be an internal memo followed by simple updates to the title on the website and on email signatures. Titles chosen to indicate the structural or symbolic priorities for the college should be the sole responsibility of the dean.

Shifting between Functional and Divisional Associate Deans

The most radical reorganization of the dean's office occurs when moving between the functional versus divisional associate dean models. This type of reorganization involves the previously described office changes along with changing the reporting lines of subordinate units. From conversations with deans who have gone through such organizational changes, it appears the movement is more often in the direction of moving from functional to divisional deans. This is associated within the increasing size and complexity of a college, as growth has been the norm at many larger institutions. Here are two examples of change from functional to divisional models and another that moved from divisional to functional.

At the University of Colorado at Boulder in 1996, a search for a new dean of the College of Arts and Sciences was initiated. At the same time, the vice chancellor of academic affairs charged an ad hoc faculty committee with reviewing the organizational structure of the College, intending to allow the incoming dean to work with the committee's findings to improve operations of the dean's office. In its report to the vice chancellor, the committee outlined its findings after assessing the current organization and the organizational models used by six other research universities, and interviewing the college's department chairs and faculty and other key university administrators.

The report focused on differentiation between functional and divisional associate dean models, concluding that the current functional structure was not actually functional in practice as the associate deans did not have budgetary or decision-making authority. This reality required the dean to spend inordinate time with transactional activities. Furthermore, due to the size of the college, responses from the dean were not timely—creating problems for department chairs and faculty.

The report included pros and cons of both models, specific to their institution. This was a key part of their analysis, as faculty and administrators could see how each model would impact them individually and collectively [Human Resource]. Since this report came from faculty and was presented from an academic (dispassionate) perspective, it largely addressed shared-governance expectations and the political aspects of the change. Therefore, any decision made by the incoming dean likely would be accepted by the faculty. Ultimately, the new dean shifted the college to a divisional dean structure.

Another approach to the limitations inherent in moving away from a functional dean structure was used by Bret Danilowicz when he settled in as dean at Oklahoma State University. In place of changing the existing functional model, he delegated and empowered associate deans with specific areas of budgetary control and decision-making authority. For example, one associate dean is now charged with overseeing the budget for contingent faculty and those staffing responsibilities, and another with overseeing the Facilities & Administrative budget and its deployment. Although they still check in with Bret on larger strategic decisions, this approach frees him to be timely in his responses to department chairs and faculty. It does not address the limitations of the functional model, but it illustrates there is flexibility within any structure to try to improve operations without going through a major structural change.

A different approach was used in the College of Arts and Sciences at Baylor University. The dean recognized some type of change was needed as the volume of work coming into the office was too much to be handled by a dean and his five associate deans. In the existing structure, there were four functional associate deans, an executive associate dean was looking after the humanities, and the dean himself was overseeing the sciences. He received approval from the provost to add staffing and make necessary organization changes to address the volume of work.

With the provost's approval for increased staffing in hand, he met with the dean of Arts and Sciences at a peer institution to discuss the divisional dean model used at his college. After conversation with a few of his department chairs, but without discussion with faculty, the dean implemented the change to an organizational structure of two divisions. The new structure shifted the existing executive associate dean to one of the new divisional dean slots, required an appointment to a new divisional associate dean position and the appointment of a new administrative assistant to the divisional associate deans. The office now totaled four functional and two divisional associate deans.

Following the change, the work of the office was more streamlined, faculty had more regular contact with the divisional deans and the dean had more time for fundraising and strategic planning. The office received little pushback from departments or faculty about the new organizational structure—although the dean received some criticism concerning how the new divisional deans were appointed.

In an example of reorganization in the opposite direction, the dean of Arts and Sciences at a small private university found the existing divisional model was becoming a hindrance to performance. The four associate deans who oversaw four divisions seemed more focused on their divisions than on outcomes for the college as a whole. Realizing that once the focus of these individuals had shifted it would be difficult to redirect, the dean changed the structure to a functional one using three associate deans, with the department heads reporting to the dean. This change removed the split focus of the leadership team, and the dean reported a better relationship with his department heads along with the associate deans being more responsive to the dean's needs. The change also removed an intermediate administrative level and made the organization chart more horizontal.

Centralizing Support Functions

Heads of departments and schools appreciate having support staff report to them. It is easy to understand why: a staff assistant proximate to one's office is preferable to one located in another building, and decisions of who best fits for positions in terms of skills and personality is up to them. So inherently, pressure exists against consolidating staff in a central office with hiring controlled by the dean's office. Some functions are decentralized by their nature, for example, students dropping by the unit office for help need to have someone present to point them in the right direction, but when functional services are decentralized (e.g., purchasing, IT, advising), workload is not distributed evenly across departments, resulting in underutilization of some staff members, or having their workload spread across so many functions that they are ineffective at some of them. The quality of those services is also variable, as the managers of those staff and faculty do not have the time or expertise to provide optimal oversight on a wide range of functions. Therefore, there can be a high fiscal and functional cost to maintaining separate services.

As Figure 2.10 (page 36) illustrates, centralized support offices for the college often emerge as the college grows in scope and complexity. This allows for the work that accumulates at uneven times across units to be averaged out by fewer staff who report to a director specialized in overseeing this type of work, increasing efficiency and effectiveness.

Most are familiar with examples of decentralizing services. Any time a new department or center is created, or departments or colleges are split, at least one staff line is assigned to the new unit, effectively decentralizing services. Following are two examples where resources were added to improve services through centralization, and one example of centralization due to budget cuts.

When Bret was a dean at Georgia Southern University, he centralized advisement services for his college. Faculty had previously advised students, but despite the time needed for the activity, they were not given any reassigned time for this service [Human Resource]. Therefore, most faculty members did not relish serving as advisors, with advisement degenerating into "course scheduling" for students. Students wrote scathing reviews of advising every year (and some even sent anonymous letters to the Governor's office about poor advising).

Colleges had been tasked with increasing student retention, progression, and graduation rate—not an uncommon exercise. A small group of administrators and faculty came together to develop a National Science Foundation (NSF) grant based on adopting best practices used by other institutions. One of the initiatives identified—based on a wealth of data—was to create a centralized "intrusive" advising model. This approach requires advising be done only by faculty who enjoyed it and are given either reassigned time or additional compensation. These faculty advisors are assisted by staff skilled in identifying students who were at risk and working with those students.

The NSF grant was funded and a staff director knowledgeable about best practices in advisement was hired. The faculty supported the change to a centralized model as they no longer had an "unfunded advising mandate" as part of their workload. The lone exception was a department with few majors that believed all the faculty should serve as advisors to help recruit students into their programs.

Within a year, an effective team of faculty and staff were enjoying their work advising students, and student feedback was supportive of the advising they were receiving. Retention and progression increased over the next few years. Although this approach requires several staff lines and the equivalent of a few faculty lines (reassigned time for faculty), additional income generated through increased retention and progression more than compensated for the investment. Permanent funds needed for the lines to replace the grant funding were later secured through the provost's office based on this argument.

So inherently, pressure exists against consolidating staff in a central office with hiring controlled by the dean's office.

Another example of centralized services requiring new investment comes from Northern Illinois University. There, the departments and the college were trying to increase their external visibility through press releases, the college website, brochures, and so forth. However, they had been trying to do so using already over-obligated faculty and staff, and the impact of the marketing effort was less than desired. The dean hoped to create a centralized service called the College Communications Group with dedicated staff including a director who specialized in these services.

The dean was sensitive about new resources going to the dean's office instead of to departments. He therefore developed the office slowly, demonstrating step-by-step the value added by it. As a first step, an ad hoc advisory group was planning and publicizing the college's 50th anniversary [Symbolic]. This advisory group morphed into a temporary office, then after another two years, into a permanent structure for which a director was hired. At each step, the quality and volume of communications about the college improved and the buy-in for the office did as well.

At the University of Alaska Anchorage, budget cuts were impending due to flat enrollments and declining state support. The dean of Arts and Sciences proposed and led a centralization of all college support services. Prior to reorganization, each department had one or two administrative assistants. Except for a few of the largest departments that retained a receptionist, all positions were reassigned and co-located to one of four divisional "shared service hubs" (arts, humanities, social sciences, sciences).

Staff members were divided among divisions equally, with each hub employing a receptionist to handle all incoming calls to any department within the division, an administrative/financial assistant to each divisional associate dean, a social media and webmaster, and a course scheduling/enrollment management/book-order assistant. Soon after implementing the change, it became apparent the service needs in all divisions were not the same, so shifting of effort among tasks has been ongoing. Centralizing into hubs was far more cost- and work-efficient, leaving ample savings for the college to add additional advising staff to the college. The co-location of staff required the dean to find the physical space for the hubs within each division.

Overall, it took a year from the onset of planning to receive approvals to implement the changes. The reorganization required terminating all staff from their current roles and encouraging them to re-apply to new positions under the hub structure. The dean realized it would be a challenge to keep staff from feeling threatened, so they would not leave preemptively for other employment [Human Resource]. He believes having a pre-commitment for unwavering support from the upper administration prior was crucial in making the shift [Political].

The Process for Reorganizing Your Office Staff

We found in our interviews with dozens of deans that almost every single one recommended new deans *take their time* when planning and implementing the kinds of changes discussed above. This is particularly true for those entering a position from outside the institution. Moving slowly in order to get to know the people, their positions, and the politics and culture of the college is time well spent. The political and symbolic frames of view may be more complex than realized at first glance. And involving others in the conversation is part of a sound shared governance process.

Table 5.1 enumerates principles that can guide you through a successful change process for your office.

Many of these principles are applicable to other administrative changes a dean might implement. Deans should also understand they have the latitude to make many of the choices about who participates, and how, while understanding that choices have political and symbolic consequences.

~ ~ ~ ~ ~ ~

After reading this chapter, you should better understand how to organize the staff and responsibilities within your office. The next chapter explores the various ways deans can organize the work of the faculty, particularly through departments, programs, centers, and schools in their college.

TABLE 5.1
Recommended Principles in Reorganizing the Dean's Office[1]

- Take your time and do not rush the process.

- Develop an agenda to outline the need for change.

- Define where you sit in the decision-making process and how the advisory/input system will work.

- If you are new to the institution, learn from knowledgeable people what the cultural norms for dialogue and change exist.

- Identify how the communication process will work, invite feedback on the process, be open to adjust it based on feedback.

- Have others help identify the problems this will address and communicate the need to address these common goals.

- Gain support for the agenda with the provost and through meetings with individuals and groups likely to influence changes.

- Bargain and negotiate authentically.

- If there is an appeal structure to these decisions, inform the faculty how it will work (and make sure your boss has agreed).

- Identify who is responsible for implementing the agreed changes.

[1] Several of these principles are adapted from Bolman and Deal (2010).

Organizing the Faculty Within a College

I'm looking at reorganizing departments within my College. Some of my questions include: What are the reasons for reorganization? How does one convey the need for reorganization to the faculty? What are the factors to consider? Metrics? Data points? What process should be followed?

—Posting to the CCAS Deans ListServ from a relatively new A&S dean

Just as new deans inherit the organization structure of the dean's office, they also come into an existing configuration for organizing academics (i.e., their faculty and programs). The organizing framework is most often a departmental structure where units are led by a chair or head and faculty are housed within traditional disciplines (such as Chemistry, Biology, Mathematics, English, Political Science, Philosophy, etc.). Sometimes related disciplines are grouped into the same department (e.g., Languages and Literature, Sociology and Anthropology, Chemistry and Physics). Such groupings are increasingly prevalent with decreasing institutional size.

Additionally, faculty work (most typically research) can be organized into centers or institutes, although institutions may use these terms differently and often interchange them. Interdisciplinary programs, research, and teaching might be housed in a center that has an administrative director, but does not have full faculty lines and therefore, faculty from established departments make up the teaching pool.

What precipitates proposals to reorganize faculty work? Any number of factors may be at play, including:

Changes initiated by faculty/departments
- A segment within a department wants to raise its visibility
- A breakdown in relations occurs between faculty within disciplinary factions

Changes initiated by the dean
- The dean perceives a better way to organize faculty work
- A change in the budget situation, particularly during periods of fiscal cutbacks

- Changes to a program (growth or shrinkage)

- A desire to encourage interdisciplinarity

- A need to address a toxic working relationship among faculty within a department

Changes initiated outside the college

- Upper administration is reorganizing the college/school structure

- A department in another college believes it would better fit in A&S

In the following vignettes, the genesis and rollout of changes often return—in one way or another—to a few essentials questions: What is the history of the departmental organization? What is the nature of the discipline? Does it have an internal disciplinary hierarchy or differences among faculty in their goals for teaching and research? How well do people within a department get along and resolve their differences? How similar are the expectations for research (and therefore the criteria for promotion and tenure)? How well does the departmental mission match the mission of its college?

For the most part, this chapter assumes departments already sit in a college and suggests ten possible scenarios for change. The examples in this chapter do not involve wholesale reorganization of the larger college or school unit. In other words, the categories and examples below are independent of an imposed merger or a forced splitting of two or more colleges at a university (which are covered in the next chapter).

Scenarios for Changing the Status Quo

1. Separating one discipline from an existing department to form a new department

Splitting a discipline or sub-discipline off from its home department to form an independent department is one of the most common ways faculty and programs are reorganized. This move can be occasioned by a number of factors: growth in the popularity of the sub-discipline; unresolvable tensions between factions within the department; emergence of a new line of research within the original discipline; or from a desire to enhance a sub-discipline which shows promise for growth. It can also become desirable when smaller disciplines housed together grow large enough to want administrative independence. Separations can be initiated by a department as a whole, by the sub-discipline, or by the dean. The following cases illustrate these situations.

a) At a small private college, the separation of a Communications program from the Department of Performing and Creative Arts was a function of its rapid growth in enrollment and faculty. This split resolved several issues existing within the department, and the two groups were happy to part ways. Most of the

Communications faculty had doctorates, while most Performing and Creative Arts faculty had M.F.A. degrees. Their sensibilities were thus different. In the end, both groups celebrated the separation.

b) A program in Theoretical Linguistics was housed within English. Over a period of years, the Linguistics faculty had decided they wanted to add a TESOL program. When the TESOL program was approved, it grew by leaps and bounds. Those teaching in the Linguistics programs—who were all English faculty—decided they could be more effective if they could have their own department. They came to the dean and convinced her to agree.

The dean required that some of them would have to move their lines from English to Linguistics, which would mean leaving a well-established large department (English) to move to a small new department. Two decided to take joint appointments, and the two most senior moved their lines fully. Since then, two new lines have been added. This restructuring occurred at a large comprehensive unionized institution, and according to the contract, faculty members can move their lines if the receiving department is willing to welcome them. The department losing the faculty member has no say.

c) When a new dean of A&S came on board, the head for the Department of Mathematical Sciences was stepping down and informed him the Computer Science faculty (included as a division within the department) had been feeling marginalized and isolated since they were in a minority and the kind of work they did was not understood by the mathematicians. They were chafing and wanted their own department. The investment in the new CS department seemed reasonable because all expected it would thrive and grow.

The dean took advantage of the department head stepping down and appointed a senior faculty member from another department (a former dean) as interim head to help oversee the division into two departments. Once the division proceeded, an outside head was hired for the new Department of Mathematics and Statistics, and then the retired dean agreed to stay for a year as the head of the new Department of Computer Science while the search for a new head commenced. As the two departments worked through the fission, they had to address issues such as restructuring governance, redoing P&T documents, and so forth. Some space was also reconfigured, and an additional staff position was hired to serve CS.

The dean believed the separation went smoothly because it came as a recommendation from the faculty, therefore no reluctance or distress existed to overcome. It was just a matter of getting the procedures in place and implementing the split. Once on its own, Computer Science benefited from having a clearer institutional identity to recruit students and from greater visibility on campus. The relations between the two groups have stayed positive.

2. Merging two or more departments into one

A move to merge two departments is often initiated for reasons similar to splitting a department: change in the popularity of a major, or unresolvable tensions between faculty (as in the two instances below). Deans may also be motivated to maintain a modicum of equity of majors and full-time faculty among departments within the college.

a) An A&S dean at a public research university became convinced a merger of two language departments might be beneficial. Over a number of years, additional faculty had been added to teach new languages in one of the departments to the extent it was becoming the "Department of Other Languages." The dean believed the faculty in one of the departments was more open to experimentation than those in the other and he hoped bringing the two groups together might generate a bit more flexibility in pedagogy.

He embarked on a series of conversations with his provost and with deans in peer institutions and looked at other campuses in the system to which his university belonged, discovering that the most common arrangement was for all languages to be in a single department. The terms of both his department heads were due to expire at the same time (two years in the future), so the timing of a merger would avoid asking for resignations.

Armed with a number of arguments to support the move, he met with the two heads separately. One head said she had been thinking along those lines herself; the head of the other department did not like the idea, as he wanted the department to retain its own identity. It took more conversation to persuade him that the dean was determined to make this change and did not find the head's arguments compelling. The head agreed not to oppose the merger. The dean met with the department heads together and suggested when their terms expired, he would go outside to hire someone so the new head would not be identified with one of the former departments.

He followed this meeting with a fairly long letter to the faculty members the move would impact, outlining his ideas as to why it was a good idea. Then he met with the combined department members and the merger was discussed for several hours. He described his approach as:

> I presented it to them as a decision I had made for the reasons outlined in my letter and that we were going to make this change. I explained that the provost was supportive as were the two department heads, and what we were talking about was the mechanism for how we would do this, not if. That was important because it was a defensible move and I didn't want to start the discussion about whether to do it.

The overall approval process went fairly smoothly, even though a few objected pretty strongly and some didn't think it the best idea in the world but couldn't come up arguments as to why not.

He believes things have gone reasonably well in the years since. After the first year, the faculty "pretty much got over it" and contributed energetically to implementing the merger. They drew up an Instrument of Governance (which had been lacking in both the original departments) as well as new tenure and promotion guidelines. As more new faculty were hired, the historical sense of connectedness to the old departments began to weaken. And in fact, some new comparative literature courses, taught in English, were created, which may not have happened when there were separate departments.

b) Within the first week of his arrival at a new institution, a dean at a comprehensive institution learned he had inherited an untenable situation in one of his departments. Tensions between two disciplinary factions within the department were exacerbated by bullying behavior. Years of festering warfare had been held at bay by a chair who had just retired. By agreement with his provost, the dean hired an outside consultant to assess the situation; based upon her findings, the dean concluded the most promising solution was to allow one subunit of faculty (Political Science) to become its own department, and to merge the other subunit (Public Administration) into a large and more stable department.

The dean identified the most logical host department and worked with the chair and her faculty to agree to accept these new colleagues. Not only would it separate former foes from each other, but it also would give the Public Administration faculty the opportunity to heal and to learn how a healthy academic unit should function. He charged the newly merged department with revising several key policies to reflect the changed situation (e.g., P&T and merit pay). The dean's intent here was to focus the two groups on developing a working relationship as well as a sense of unity. But as the policies became wrapped up in petty battles, he laid down a firm deadline for completing the tasks. When no agreements were achieved by the deadline, he asked the provost for permission to impose policies on the unit until acceptable policies were produced. The dean reported:

> Most animosity was now redirected toward me—and new policies were crafted within a month. The environment was not perfect but more cooperation ensued, perhaps in fear of what the awful dean would do next! Things are now smooth, and everyone seems to be talking with one another, including to me.

3. **Moving a department from another college/school into A&S**

As the following cases illustrate, departments from another college may become incorporated into the A&S college due to a shake-up of colleges outside A&S, or when a department housed in another college believes it would be better served within A&S. Full buy-in from the provost is required to make this kind of change work.

a) A new chancellor and provost decided they wanted to combine two existing professional schools, both which were fairly small. One of the schools had an Interior Architecture program. As this idea evolved, the head of Interior Architecture came to the A&S dean to say the department was going to request it be moved into the College of Arts and Sciences. Although it is a professional program, the dean could see some advantages to the College to having them join. The dean said he was open to the idea and would meet with the provost to see if he approved. The provost, it turned out, was delighted with this idea because the merger of the two professional schools was meeting with opposition and, in his mind, if any department was willing to move somewhere, he would be pleased.

The dean next embarked on a deliberate set of steps that involved 1) introducing the idea to his Administrative Council for a discussion (no objections), 2) having the department head come to the Admin Council and talk to them (very cordial meeting), and 3) meeting with the departmental faculty to describe what the College of Arts & Sciences was like and how business was conducted. "It was a matter of having all the right conversations and getting to know each other," says the dean.

> And then we worked on the process—we got the budget officer involved, decided on the various steps needed to make the move… it all went very smoothly. They really have been a great benefit to the College. One of the things that was coincidental was that a couple years previously a new building had been built for them and the Art program (in A&S), so they were already sharing some space and facilities and collaborating across Colleges. I had hired a new head in the Art Department who got along well with the head of Interior Architecture. Both are studio-based programs that make heavy use of computer technology, and a single IT person supports both departments.

b) At a large research university, the chair of a department that included an accredited program started conversations with the provost as a result of being somewhat dissatisfied with being in the School of Professional Studies. Things took off from there, with "a lot of back and forth, with the provost, with the A&S dean, the dean of the School of Professional Studies—who was not in favor but was not able to stop it," according to a university dean.

When it was finally decided the department would come into the CAS (College of Arts & Sciences), many changes needed to happen: change in course numbers, curriculum, admission requirements, and certification of degrees. There were changes in the way the department—its programs and courses—had to go through the CAS and other bureaucratic processes. Several meetings with the stakeholders helped to determine what processes had to be carried out to conform to practices in CAS. The dean relates:

> One of the other things is that here in the CAS, we have a liberal arts core that all of our students follow, which was different from the core of the School of Professional Studies. The first year was a bit tricky, especially advising their students because their faculty had to be integrated into our process, especially in understanding the core.

Once the change occurred, the chair said the department was much happier in CAS and they felt they had better resources and were aligned with the culture of CAS. They feel the liberal arts background their students are getting in A&S is better than was the case in their former school. "It was a happy marriage into A&S," believes the dean.

4. **Moving a department from A&S into another existing college/school**

   For historical reasons, an A&S college may include a program better fitted to the mission and scholarly research framework of a professional school. Unless faculty members in a program are discontent, moving the program into another college or school requires a deft approach by the dean. The deans involved in the following cases did so successfully.

a) At a large southern public university, the College of Science and Mathematics included a program in Print Management. It was the dean's perception it simply did not fit with the rest of the College because of its focus on service to the printing industry. As things evolved, it looked to be a good fit with the Graphic Design program (housed in the College of Liberal Arts & Social Sciences), which also was more focused on professional service. The two deans started a conversation about making the change. Then they organized a social event to bring faculty members together over the idea. Through continued discussion among the faculty, their chairs, and the deans (and keeping the provost in the loop), the faculty agreed they might be better able to create interdisciplinary teaching and research opportunities for themselves and their students if they were co-located and administered. Print Management, along with its faculty and space, moved to the Department of Graphic Design. This new location has proven to be a better fit.

b) A dean at a large private university was in conversation with the head of her Biology department about whether its Nutrition program was a good fit with the goals of the department. The Biology Department was research-focused, winning grants from the National Institute of Health (NIH) and the National Science Foundation (NSF), and it aimed to propel its students into graduate and medical school or into technician jobs. The faculty in Nutrition, on the other hand, were receiving small contracts from school systems and health departments about how to teach nutrition to school children and were training graduates to become Registered Dieticians. It seemed clear to the two of them that Nutrition was not an appropriate discipline for the department. For the dean, the program's focus was not consistent with the larger goals of the College of Arts and Sciences.

She met with her counterpart in the College of Nursing and Health Professions, an application-focused program. She explained to the other dean the goals of the Nutrition program; the Nursing and Health Professions dean agreed Nutrition was consistent with what they were doing and, importantly, the College of Nursing and Health Professions was cognizant of not doing enough about issues of healthy eating and obesity. The timing for such a move seemed propitious.

Together the deans went to the provost who agreed it sounded logical, but asked what they planned to do about the faculty, considering two were tenured and two were pre-tenure. As explained by the A&S dean,

> We [the two deans] both believe in doing a lot of talking before action, so that's the approach we took. We both met with the Nutrition faculty as a whole and separately. After this consultation, we agreed we would just switch tenure homes for the two tenured faculty members and for the pre-tenures, we would review the guidelines, and see if it would do them a disservice to move.

To ensure these two professors were not disadvantaged by the move, a joint committee was named to clarify expectations for tenure. The committee clarified why these faculty had focused more on research while in Biology, rather than on application as emphasized in the Nursing & Health Professions criteria. Subsequently, both faculty members were awarded tenure. Today, the dean reports that whereas the program had been "invisible" in Biology, it is now "vibrant and flourishing."

5. **Creating a new school out of existing departments**
   Sometimes it makes sense to pull together a cluster of departments into a new school within a college or into an entirely new college. As these two cases illustrate, there is the perception that being an independent school or college will give more visibility and voice to a disciplinary cluster. Other reasons include using the school framework as a testing ground for whether it should eventually become an independent college; to allow for promotion and tenure guidelines better suited to those disciplines (e.g., creative or applied scholarship rather than research); and to bring efficiencies in staffing, event planning, and the like.

a) At a public comprehensive university, four departments (Art, Communication & Media, Music, Theatre & Dance) within the College of Liberal Arts were combined into a School of Arts, Media and Communication. When the idea initially arose, the faculty in the other four departments in the College were not enthusiastic, but the faculty in the arts felt that becoming a school within the college would be beneficial for a number of reasons, including

- both the faculty and members of the surrounding community wished to enhance the visibility of what was going on in the Fine Arts;

- during a review of the College's P&T guidelines, it became apparent those four areas were very different from the rest of the college. Having a separate category of "creative activity" rather than "research" for faculty in a separate school would better fit those fields; and

- being combined into a school would create synergy among the faculty.

Implementation of the change was not without challenges. There was precedent at the University for departments to split off into schools, with the upper administration sanctioning various levels of independence: a school can stay in its college, become a college on its own, or become its own school. In this case, the first approach was approved, but no director would be named. The dean would serve as the school director.

Currently, the faculty meets either as the College of Liberal Arts (four departments) or the School of Arts, Media, and Communication (four departments). The relatively new dean has asked the chairs if it would be a good idea to all meet together each fall. He also reports:

> We struggle with branding ourselves, but I don't know how we will
> resolve this until we have a director. We need to be raising our profile in
> the community with our performances and exhibitions. Right now we're
> in a holding pattern without a director. Once this happens and we get our
> own Fine Arts building, things may change.

b) The School of Arts and Sciences (SOAS) of a small Midwestern institution generated two-thirds of the credit hours on campus, with the other four schools generating the remaining third. There was a sense SOAS was too large in proportion to the size of the other schools. Science faculty felt it would be in their best interest in the long term to have their own school. They also felt science was different enough from other parts of A&S that they could better advocate and represent their own interests if they were on their own. Finally, they believed a separate and smaller school of sciences would allow them to be more flexible and visible in order to enhance the identity of the natural sciences, mathematics, and informatics on campus. The science faculty voted among themselves to request a reorganization of A&S; they then brought it to the dean, who supported it. This was followed by a schoolwide meeting, characterized as "very amicable," where the proposal to reorganize into two schools was approved unanimously.

At the time, SOAS was under an interim dean, a former dean who had come out of retirement to serve. "This may have helped," relates one of the faculty leaders, "because then we're not talking about changing someone's job here." And at the same time, "we had a chancellor who was willing to shake things up. So they were more accommodating to change than otherwise might have been the case."

The schoolwide vote took place in January, with the reorganization to take effect the following July 1. There began a "soft split" in the intervening months, overseen by the interim dean. The change was not too complex as departments retained their budgets and items that were schoolwide (travel, copying) were split proportionately based upon the number of faculty. Each department also had its own P&T guidelines, which did not change under the reorganization.

By several measures, the reorganization has been successful, with both schools (the new School of Sciences and the remaining school, now called Humanities and Social Sciences) experiencing enrollment gains. The dean of the School of Sciences believes the independent school status has given them more opportunities to promote programs and activities in the sciences. For instance, it is helpful during the budget development process to have one voice speaking on behalf of the School of Sciences rather than speaking as a subset of Arts and Sciences.

6. **Creating programs, centers, and institutes**
    With the rise in interdisciplinary research, teaching, and programs, faculty and deans often establish centers or institutes as the organizing framework for these cross- or multi-disciplinary endeavors. Whether to house research efforts, programs or courses, deans often must get involved to sort out the thorny issues of faculty workload, peer evaluation, and management oversight. These three cases encompass instances where courses, programs, and/or research were at play.

a) As part of the process of developing a university-level strategic plan at a Midwestern research university, faulty were invited to submit 1-2 page "concept papers," with either wholly- or partially-formed ideas welcomed. In reviewing all the proposals, the A&S dean found a strong cluster of faculty ideas around the general idea of environmental studies. The proposals reflected competing agendas, with some wanting a pure research center, and others suggesting a new academic program be established. The dean, along with the provost's staff, merged programmatic elements together starting with a new undergraduate degree, which was an institutional priority.

Because there was a formal strategic planning process, new funding was available, which served to catalyze the initiative. The new Environmental Studies Center was able to launch vigorously because of the coupling of faculty enthusiasm and institutional support and investment. The undergraduate major in Environmental Studies was developed quickly after getting approvals at the institutional and system level. The degree program itself runs on a small core of ES courses and basically builds the rest of the curriculum on what exists within the other disciplines. Within an environment of financial contraction, these students are filling seats that otherwise might be empty. "Creating this center has pulled faculty together on the research side," says the dean.

Faculty self-identified to be in the Center; then as they codified operational rules among themselves, they defined who would qualify as a member. It did not make organizational sense to form a department because the center is comprised of a small core of joint appointments and 25-30 faculty members in other departments who wanted to be involved.

The dean attributes the success of the Center to the faculty's ability to self-organize around a common interest. "They naturally wanted to come together; their passion for the issue has taken this a long way down the road. Many faculty care about this and want to be involved." Now the Center has a director, a cost center, a budget, protocols, and some control over its faculty. "It's almost a department. The director is virtually indistinguishable from a chair at this point," according to the dean.

b) A dean of A&S at a research institution perceived considerable dissatisfaction among various departments who were contributing faculty and other resources to a major in International Area Studies and to minors in Africana Studies, Women and Gender Studies, and Judaic Studies. The dean also was concerned about inefficiency and inconsistency across these programs that included: each of the minors in a different department, with differing expectations of support from office staff; often the number of students enrolled in a course was the minimum required; there was no course sharing among the minors; and sponsored events often conflicted with each other.

Believing in the importance of these programs for the students and community members, the dean decided to establish the infrastructure to create a Center for Interdisciplinary Programs under which these programs would be housed. She provided funding for two new positions: one in outreach and event planning; the other in finance and budget support. An advisor position transferred from the International Area Studies program, and the directors of the program would take turns rotating the responsibilities of the Center director. An office suite was identified to house the director and three staff positions.

As hoped, this move allowed the directors to coordinate their activities on several fronts:

- Course offerings were reviewed for overlap and compatibility, resulting in a single research methods course for all students and acceptance of electives across the programs

- Student advising could be handled by one person across all programs

- Events (speakers and conferences) were coordinated and co-sponsored, resulting in increased attendance and reduced costs

- One person—the outreach coordinator—represented all the programs to the broader community

c) Soon after coming on the job, an A&S dean learned her faculty who specialized in plant science had entered into discussions with faculty members in the College of Agriculture to try to bring together all those interested in collaborative research in the field. The faculty believed synergy between the research they were conducting and the applied focus of research in Agriculture would be beneficial to everyone.

The dean and her counterpart in the College of Ag agreed to fund a seminar series under a "Plant Research Center" to feature the work of a member of the faculty or an outside expert. Ideally, learning about each other's work would lead to collaborative grant proposals, which "is what gets funded these days." The faculty decided to hold the seminars over lunch in a neutral location, and the effort has proven not only popular but has indeed led to cross-college collaboration and grant awards.

The deans further supported this initiative by providing seed grants (around $5,000-$8,000) for collecting data that could then serve as baseline work for grant proposals. The faculty also submitted a proposal for an NSF graduate fellow training grant. The deans expect to continue funding the Center until such time as it generates sufficient F&A to become self-supporting. Staff support is provided by the cooperating departments.

7. **Reorganizing from disciplinary clusters into departments**

A few colleges use disciplinary clusters rather than traditional departments as the organizing framework for all majors and programs. Some small colleges (as illustrated by the following case) find that disciplinary clusters no longer work when enrollment grows and faculty increases. Relying upon chairs to provide leadership to disciplines in which they have no background is most problematic.

In 2005-2006, the administration at a medium-sized private liberal-arts institution raised the idea of changing from its current configuration of five (5) schools housing related faculty and programs and headed by deans, to establishing departments with chairs within those schools. At the time, each discipline had an area coordinator whose basic responsibility was scheduling.

The university was growing rapidly in terms of students and faculty, and the lack of departments headed by chairs placed an untenable burden on the deans, who were responsible for the hiring and evaluation of all faculty and directing all assessment efforts and program reviews. In 2005, for instance, the School of Humanities housed 12 disciplines offering 14 majors and 20 minors (with 70 fulltime faculty and 750+ majors). After a process lasting several years, the School of Humanities is now constituted of seven (7) departments, each with its own chair. Three of the largest of the original 12 areas became independent departments; the other nine were merged into four newly named departments that combined two or more related disciplines. Similar reconfigurations played out in the other A&S schools.

The dean of humanities attributes the success of this change to making it a faculty-based process that was not rushed. Consideration was given to necessary changes to the Faculty Manual regarding issues such as the role of the chairs in faculty evaluation, to the naming of the founding chairs who are now being given released time and compensation for the new duties, and to funding for chair training.

8. **Reorganizing departments into disciplinary clusters/schools**

Merging departments into clusters (and doing away with the departments) had a short heyday a few years back when deans and provosts viewed this as a way to "break down the silos" between disciplinary faculty. The other reason this move is popular is budgetary (as seen in the case below), as it reduces the monetary support (mainly in the form of release time) necessary to support multiple chairs.

At a medium-sized comprehensive institution, a university-wide reorganization in 2012 was driven by the need to address a substantial budget shortfall over a 12-month period. Within Arts and Sciences, this led to the consolidation of fourteen departments into four schools (each comprised of faculty in related disciplines) within the College. Each school is now led by a director (the budget unit head, with responsibilities similar to those of a department chair) and an associate director. The director, as leader of the school, is responsible for managing the school's budget and for the annual evaluations of faculty and staff in the school. Each degree program has a coordinator who serves essentially as a point-person for faculty and students. The director and associate director each have a two-course reduction and receive a small administrative stipend. The coordinator has a one-course reduction, but does not earn a stipend. For P&T, the first level of review is conducted by faculty in the applicant's field. Then the school director, not the program coordinator, reviews the portfolio at the second level.

Faculty generally understood the change and agreed it was better to make ends meet by reorganizing the College than by eliminating degree programs. It helped the College address a substantial part of the budget shortfall (because fewer administrative stipends and administrative course releases had to be awarded) and it provided for a more effective running of the College and its programs. Bringing similar programs together under one school umbrella also provided greater opportunities for cross-collaboration. A weakness of the model, reports the associate dean, is "many faculty feel their programs have lost some of their identity. They identify more with, say, the biology program than with the School of Sciences."

9. **Keeping two departments separate under a single chair and support staff**

Although not a frequent occurrence, as this case demonstrates, assigning a single chair to oversee two separate departments may solve the problem of a leadership vacuum. At a Midwestern research university, no one in the relatively small computer science department wanted to become the new chair, and the dean lacked the resources for an outside hire. He considered solving the problem by merging CS into Mathematics (from which is separated a few years prior) but received pushback from faculty in both departments. Over the intervening years, they had formed their own identities and could not see the benefit of again being under one roof. The dean proposed keeping the departments separate, but placing the same chair over them (for which he raised the compensation by $5000) and sharing support staff. This fix was put in place, saving administrative costs.

Each department maintained its own committees and operating procedures and adjusted quite easily to the change. "I believe a lot of this satisfaction has to do with the chair," writes the dean, "as she has really created a sense of direction and home for all of them." This approach has the potential to fail if it is perceived the chair shows favoritism in areas such as resource allocation toward one department over another.

10. **Moving faculty from one department to another**

Sometimes circumstances arise that result in a shortage of faculty in a discipline or when an individual faculty member believes he or she is better fit with a different program. But few faculty wish to change disciplines, and, for those who do, departments are loath to relinquish a faculty member as a faculty line often exists with them. The following case illustrates how a dean and his faculty arrived at a solution addressing the need for faculty dedicated to teaching in an interdisciplinary program.

A medium-sized comprehensive university had been experiencing difficulty growing interdisciplinary programs that build on the expertise of existing faculty because their home departments were reluctant to allow their faculty to teach outside their departments. Under the dean's leadership, a procedure was developed for how to reallocate faculty lines internally that allowed a reallocation of a portion of a faculty member's line to other areas of the College by providing replacements to the "giving" department, with the dean's approval. For example, the Global Studies major had been growing quickly but lacked senior faculty appointments. The dean granted Global Studies a growth hire and the line was "traded" to Political Science in exchange for 50 percent of two senior faculty members' lines. The dean considered this solution "a win-win."

Additional considerations

Even enumerating the ten categories above, numerous variations remain for how to organize faculty work. A new department could be created out of whole cloth (rather than as an offshoot of an existing department) when a university decides to launch a new degree program. Several Land Grant institutions cite examples of A&S "sharing" a department with the College of Agriculture or Engineering. Occasionally colleges attempt to organize all the departments into schools within the college.

It is worth noting that, in gathering examples, we found that what gets done does not necessarily stay done. Departmental mergers fall apart; departments once separated may come back together; a cluster of programs becomes a school within the college later becomes an independent school or college; or a new interdisciplinary center later becomes a department.

Effective Processes to Encourage and Facilitate Buy-in to Change

As the examples above illustrate, a number of circumstances provide opportunity for changing how faculty work is organized. The question remains what processes should be attended to in order to maximize the chance for successful resolution and implementation.

Consider the extent to which the Four Frames provide guidance in this regard. In interviews and in postings on the CCAS ListServ, deans often use language reflecting the four frames when relating how they went about making changes to departmental structures. It is unlikely most deans consciously considered each one of the frames during the change process, but as the descriptions that follow illustrate, many deans act intuitively to incorporate these considerations when deciding whether to effectuate change, when analyzing the climate for change, or when reflecting upon processes they used that proved to be effective.

Structural (the rules, policies, procedures, roles, and assignments that set contexts and boundaries for how a dean can act):

- At the small university where the science faculty initiated a split from the humanities and social sciences to form its own school, several parties agreed it was useful that the university system, of which this institution is a part, has clear policies for the steps and approvals required to create a new school.

- A dean came up with a solution for how to incentivize departments to allow members of their faculty to teach courses in an interdisciplinary program. The arrangements he put in place seems to be working well, he reports, and he believes: "what is important is that there is an MOU in place for each of these jointly appointed faculty and that the faculty, chairs, and dean are all in agreement and communicative." The Memorandum of Understanding serves as a structural agreement among the parties.

- Reflecting upon why a new interdisciplinary institute (which includes an undergraduate program) has been successful, the dean stated: "A key part of how we structure the Institute is that we have Faculty Associates (who are voluntary from other departments) and we also have joint appointments, with half their line in the Institute and the other in a traditional department, since they have to hold a line in a traditional discipline. These people are the backbone of the Institute. Our goal with making joint appointments is that there should be no advantage or disadvantage to having a joint appointment."

- In describing what was important during a tumultuous period of reducing the number of colleges at her institution, which required many departments to be relocated, the dean recommended:

  > Make sure that each dean has institutional data about each discipline, everything from average class size, credit hours generated, adjuncts versus FT – you need to know the data now before making changes. Make sure everyone has the data, otherwise you go on whatever your perceptions are – which may be outdated. Second, before you go through a lot of change, having that data will help people see the health of the institution, where the enrollments are, what's not going so well – they can have views and conversations about it. The faculty and the chairs in your college need to understand the full picture.

In short, deans are well served by starting any change process knowing the rules, procedures, and as much of the context as can be obtained. Syracuse University, for instance, has a governance document entitled *Guidelines for Addressing Major Issues* that is to be used when making significant organizational changes (see Appendix C). The University of Maryland Baltimore County established its *Criteria and Process for Formation of a School from an Existing Unit within a College at UMBC* (Appendix D). The University of Arizona's *"Merger Guidelines (Phase 1 – Preliminary Discussions and Phase 2 – Implementation)* provides detailed guidance for deans, directors, and department chairs who are considering merging any academic units (Appendix E).

If deans do not have a specified change policy to follow, it is still advisable that they establish how the change process will play out. For instance, one dean who orchestrated a merger of two departments described the process he used: "I named a steering committee to plan the merger, headed by one of my associate deans not in the department, to plan the mechanisms – new governance, P&T, etc., and it was a two-year process. Year 1: planning, Year 2: more planning and search for a new head."

In a different aspect of attending to the structural frame, the implications of change to reorganizing faculty work must be front and center once the process gets moving. Will the change involve:

- Costs to make the change and budget implications once implemented?

- Determining where faculty members have tenure?

- Review of existing P&T guidelines?

- Review of faculty governance?

- Revising of program requirements?

- A new approach to student advising?

- A MOU if the change requires cooperation among various parties?

One dean advises: "Bring in as many stakeholders as possible. If you have enough people at the table, someone is going to think of everything that needs to be changed." Don't underestimate what needs to be attended to," says another. "There's a remarkable amount of work involved in doing this kind of thing!"

Political (the dynamics of influence, power, and relationships):

- When considering whether to separate two sub-disciplines into separate departments, a dean knew it was important to keep his provost in the loop. "I was in touch with the provost along the way, as is my habit, making sure of such things as, Is she supportive of the move? Have we discussed what the resource issues are? Could I get more resources from her office if needed? My approach [with the provost] has always been to say, 'If I can work this out within the college, will you approve it?'"

- The dean described how he built support behind-the-scenes for the merging of several language departments—an idea that the dean initiated for a number of reasons: "I had laid the groundwork for this meeting [of both departments] by talking privately to four or five faculty members whom I suspected would support the idea and who were moderately influential and salted the mine a little bit. I told them, 'I would appreciate you voicing your support for this.'"

- Several deans also mention under "lessons learned" that the dynamics of new configurations among faulty must be attended to after the change is implemented. A dean who had authorized a subunit of faculty to split from its larger department to form an independent program relays: "I had to have long talks with the senior faculty [in the new program] about the need to make sure the newly hired faculty don't get caught up in the old battles between the two units." Advises another dean, "Create a definite timeline for the change to happen plus plans to review and revise—and then actually do it."

Human Resource (how people feel and what needs they seek to have satisfied):

- In considering a desired but "forced" merger of three disciplines, the dean realized: "There are unequal incentives to join together into a new department. Theatre faculty need a home and are desperate not to have to teach Gen Ed for the rest of their careers. But because the other two departments are thriving, those faculty perceive no benefit from merging with a weaker discipline. As dean, I feel that if people aren't equally appointed with a real stake in the new configuration, it just won't take." At this writing, the merger has yet to take place.

- The psychology faculty greatly desired to be separated from a department that also housed faculty from sociology, anthropology, and social work. They felt that being part of a multi-disciplinary department inhibited their ability to develop an identity and worked against them when applying for grants. Faculty in the other disciplines felt they were being abandoned and believed the department would be weaker for the separation. "After much debate, they relented" said the dean. "I persuaded them that, as in a marriage, you cannot force people to stay when they want to go off on their own."

- In considering whether to support a subunit of faculty within an Ethnic Studies department to separate off into its own department, the dean said she realized: "that these battles between the (faculty in area A and faculty in area B) are really battles about identity and history, and they were divisive. Operating in separate departments means they can leave these battles behind."

- In facilitating the move of a department from another school into his College, one dean reported: "It was important to give [the faculty in that department] the feeling that they were being welcomed into the College, the value we see that they would bring to the College, and that we could work out any problems."

- One dean described how "faculty from 'area A' felt thwarted by the faculty from 'area B'. Once separated, both departments have thrived. "Being given responsibility for their own futures and not spending time negotiating with the other 'side' has freed them both."

If there is one dominant frame in making organizational change, it is the importance of attending to "the human factor," particularly people's sense of how they feel about the proposed change. We like to believe faculty members are motivated by rationality, but in truth they are like all other people and their feelings matter a great deal. They will ask: "How is this going to affect me/my program?"

Acknowledging this aspect of affect, many deans we interviewed describe a process they used similar to this dean's description: "We held committee meetings throughout the year, held a focus session with students, and met with different constituencies." "Don't rush or appear to mandate," cautions another dean. "Give everyone the chance to weigh in." "Take the time to explain why. You can never explain enough. Explain even to those who will never be won over."

Symbolic (the need to give larger meaning to change):
- A dean of Arts and Sciences pulled three departments (Music, Theatre, and Art) together under an umbrella program, the School of Visual & Performing

Arts. "The reason this was done was that because, while the three departments are all within A&S, each independently organized its own advertising, calendaring … we looked so Mickey Mouse! Other universities have organized their arts programs into schools and they looked so much more professional than us. By forming this umbrella group, the departments could put out their communications under a unified school of the arts. There has been no change in staffing, faculty, or budgets; it's just a marketing exercise. This was a symbolic move, to signal 'We are organized.' Now the departments have a common calendar and collaboratively advertise their events."

Attending to the symbolic frame points to the need to highlight and even celebrate the change. A dean can attend a meeting of the new or reconfigured unit/s to wish them well. The university communications office can write a piece about the success of the reconfiguration. At a college faculty meeting, individual faculty who were instrumental in helping bring about the change can be recognized and thanked.

Still, Things Can Go Wrong!

Even when a dean attends to all the frames and uses the right processes, things may not go smoothly.

- A dean has attempted to broker moving Communication Sciences and Disorders into the School of Education, but the faculty have maintained resistance and the move has not gone forward.

- There was a proposal to merge theatre (with few majors) with film studies (a thriving department) and add New Media to create an Oxford-comma enforced department. The film faculty saw no benefit of merger while theatre faculty worried that they would be relegated to teaching service courses only. With no incentive to offer either faction, discussions grew toxic. Neither side listened to the other side.

- A relatively new dean attempted to reformat three biology-related departments into one or two departments. He had garnered compelling arguments and data justifying the change. He was, however, ultimately undercut by the provost despite keeping her informed in the process and securing her approval in advance.

- The idea of merging two social science programs with overlapping research and pedagogical goals into a single department surfaced and gained support among faculty from the existing departments. The move was approved up through the presidential level. A deliberative process resulted in an agreement signed by both departments that the merger would occur once a mutually acceptable chair was identified through an external search. The dean appointed a joint search committee with co-chairs (one from each department), and the committee's work concluded with recommending a qualified candidate to the dean. Unfortunately, a sub-faction of one of the departments began agitating against the merger, which soured the negotiations. The leading candidate withdrew, and even though the dean was well aware the opportunity had been lost, he sent the issue back to the faculty for reconsideration.

• The A&S dean of an urban research university believed "the silos needed to be torn down" between six loosely related disciplines. With little genuine consultation or discussion with faculty, he eliminated the departments, dismantled the administrative structure for the programs, and put all the faculty into a new school within the college. A coordinator was named for each graduate and undergraduate program but was given no teaching reduction or real authority; faculty met as a whole, but not within their disciplines; and schoolwide P&T procedures were rewritten so committees were comprised of members from multiple disciplines.

    This structure change was fraught with problems. Within a few years, faculty realigned themselves for purposes of recruiting and advising students, to develop new courses, and to make hiring decisions. A new dean agreed that many decisions needed to be handled within academic disciplines and began allowing hiring of new faculty for specific disciplines, relocating faculty offices into disciplinary clusters, and increasing the compensation and authority of the program heads.

~ ~ ~ ~ ~ ~

This chapter illustrates various ways deans and faculty can reorganize within a college, which sometimes involves cooperation and change among other colleges in the university. But what happens when a dean learns "the powers that be" are contemplating reorganizing his or her college—or even the entire university? Chapter 7 offers several case studies on how these moves may impact deans.

7

Understanding and Implementing Mandated Reorganizations

It is not necessary to change. Survival is not mandatory.
—*W. Edwards Deming*

Unexpectedly, the college president calls and says that she would like to meet with you, the provost, and another dean. At the meeting, you learn the president wants to merge your college with the other college; the provost nods in agreement. The president leaves it up to you and the dean of the other college to "work out the details" and calls out as you leave: "The new college needs to be in place in six months!"

If you are thinking: "This scenario would never happen!" or, "This kind of change is impossible to accomplish in that time frame," you would be wrong.

Mandates from the campus executive office to reshuffle academic colleges are more common than you might think. And such requests appear to be on the rise. Many of your decanal colleagues who have experienced this process were willing to share their tales with us for this book.

This chapter describes situations where campus executives decide to split or to combine colleges, and where governing bodies split or combine entire campuses. Relevance to one or more of the Four Frames is noted in brackets. The reader will learn both good practices and explore missteps taken by deans in such situations. Even if you are fortunate enough to serve in a college that can determine its own organizational structure, after reading this chapter you will be better prepared to mentor or empathize with a decanal colleague whose college's organizational structure was selected for them.

Is a Unified College of Arts and Sciences the Only Way to Go?

As discussed in Chapter 1, approximately two-thirds of the 500+ CCAS member colleges and universities organize their Arts and Sciences departments in a single college; the remaining third are organized under two or more colleges. However, just because most colleges are organized as a "combined unit" does not indicate that it is optimal.

Academic and administrative leaders and governing bodies grapple with defining an organizational structure that best meets the needs of Arts and Sciences departments as well as meeting the vision of their institution. Historically, the liberal arts (the trivium and quadrivium) functioned as the foundation of Westernized higher education. As institutions grew, Arts and Sciences were organized into a college(s) distinct from newer colleges with applied or professional emphases.

Debates about the centrality of the Arts and Sciences are not new. In 1967, the Board of Directors of CCAS recognized the challenges of creating an effective structure to meet the diverse needs of Arts and Sciences departments. CCAS noted that college reorganizations were underway at Kentucky, Michigan State, Ohio State, and Rutgers universities and sent this position statement to NASULGC (formerly the National Association of State Universities and Land-Grant Colleges, now the Association of Public and Land-grant Universities, or APLU):

> A survey of the administrative changes already proposed or adopted indicates that a particular organization structure for any institution may require unique features in response to such factors as the history of the institution, special or local objectives, the time at which changes are made, and even the geographical relations of its academic unit. Such a survey also indicates that other factors may tend even more strongly to influence the resulting organization, among them narrowing of focus within separate disciplines on individual campuses, increasing attention to graduate and professional students, and an emphasis on research. While the Commission applauds the limitation of fields in order to achieve the depth sometimes necessary to new discoveries and admires the better preparation of graduate students which often results, it sees these are significant but not controlling factors to be considered in determining the administrative organization of a state university or land-grant college. An exclusive emphasis on these may too easily lead to an administrative structure so designed that fragmentation of the liberal education of undergraduates is inevitable.

> Thus the Commission recommends to the presidents of NASULGC institutions that in undertaking a review of the administrative structures involving the arts and sciences on their campuses *they insist that the enhancement of the liberal education of undergraduates be the principle goal of the resulting structures and that the final plans be such as to insure the faculty and administration of the liberal education programs full support in carrying out their responsibilities.* [italics added].[1]

---

[1] Resolution passed at the Business Meeting at the November 1967 CCAS Annual Meeting.

This statement—now 50 years old—was a pragmatic recommendation from deans of Arts and Sciences who believed that their colleges' contribution to the liberal arts was more important than all other considerations. They recommended to keep the liberal arts central in higher education curriculum.

Today, the focus of deans of Arts and Sciences is different. Not a single institution—despite the large number of institutions we researched and the numerous leaders we interviewed—stated that enhancing liberal education was its primary goal around reorganization. Only a few even mentioned it. In fact, improving the student experience overall was rarely referred to. This seems remarkable as students are the primary reason for the existence of higher education.

Not a single institution—despite the large number of institutions we researched and the numerous leaders we interviewed—stated that enhancing liberal education was its primary goal around reorganization.

With the apparent increase in frequency of reorganizing Arts and Sciences colleges on campuses, and now knowing that the student experience is not usually considered, there are many questions a dean needs to consider. Are reorganizations a demonstration of leadership skills to the campus community (i.e., chest-pounding or CV building)? Or, as higher education evolves, is there substance behind these reorganization decisions? Exploring these questions, this chapter offers case examples of colleges splitting or merging, including the merger of colleges of two different institutions.

Context of these examples

The cases recounted here are from deans, associate deans, and provosts who have been through college reorganizations. Thus, these descriptions may possess biases and may not capture events perfectly. Furthermore, the stated reasons for the reorganization are the ones known to the deans and likely the public. It is possible decision-makers revealed only part of the story.

In one instance, rather than firing a dean not liked by the provost, executive leaders combined two colleges, conveniently finding themselves in need of only one dean and thereby avoided direct conflict. Conversely, cronyism can come into play: An executive leader could split a college, finding need for a dean who is a colleague from a former institution. Our point is that readers understand the drivers for change explained below as the stated rationales for change, but might not tell the whole story.

Although the cases below focus on colleges comprised of Arts and Sciences programs—exclusively or in some combination with non-Arts and Sciences programs—they apply to any type of college. We are aware of changes in business, education, and human science colleges that follow these same story lines. These cases do not address reorganizations based on accreditation requirements (e.g., AACSB-accredited business schools, CEPH-accredited public health schools).

Please note that the genders, names of colleges, and other details have been altered in the following case studies, as they are tangential to understanding why and how changes occurred. But additionally, we wanted (as much as possible) to protect people from potential political fallout. In all but the first case, the names of individuals, institutions, and dates are not included.

Splitting Colleges into Two or More Colleges

These first cases involve dividing a single college into two more colleges, or moving a significant segment of a college from one college to another (i.e., the college of origin will perceive a "split" while the receiving college will perceive a "merger").

Case: A rose by any other name, revisited

At Georgia Southern University, Bret was dean of the Allen E. Paulson College of Science & Technology. It housed the sciences, mathematics, and engineering technology programs. At the time, Georgia Institute of Technology, commonly known as Georgia Tech, held a monopoly on state engineering programs, enforced by the state Board of Regents. The faculty and administrators at Georgia Southern had been trying to break this monopoly for 25 years. They knew this would involve converting their existing engineering technology programs into pure engineering programs.

The president made the decision to again try to convert these programs. Other research universities possessed stand-alone colleges of engineering and the president aspired to look like them. The president also believed having a distinct college of engineering was a signal to the nation that Georgia Southern was indeed a quality institution, and that the institution had grown beyond its normal-school origins and deserved recognition as an impactful doctoral-research university. If the degree changes were approved by state authorities, he intended to split off departments from their current STEM college and create a new stand-alone engineering college. Thus, the stated rationale for reorganizing colleges was largely symbolic [Symbolic].

When the reorganization was proposed, the engineering faculty and department chairs were pleased because they been advocating for this change for a long time. The dean was also excited by the opportunity because the campus felt like the underdogs. They wanted to bring down the barricade set up by the top research university.

But beyond the enthusiasm about the symbolism of reorganization, no one was really reflecting on what the college reorganization would mean. Surprisingly little discussion about the potential reorganization occurred on campus. Faculty from non-engineering departments in the College voiced no concerns. No one seemed to hold reservations.

When the state Board of Regents approved the change to engineering programs, the president announced the degrees would be implemented the following fall (nine months away) and the college reorganization would be effective at the start of the following fiscal year (19 months away). After his initial statement, however, the president changed his plan. Instead of a stand-alone engineering college, the engineering programs would all be merged into the existing College of Information Technology, which was struggling with declining enrollments and had an interim dean. The college would be renamed the College of Engineering and Information Technology, with engineering listed first. The president said that anticipated growth in engineering programs would offset the enrollment challenges facing the current information technology programs, and the colleges overall would appear more balanced and productive to the Board of Regents [Political].

But beyond the enthusiasm about the symbolism of reorganization, no one was really reflecting on what the college reorganization would mean.

The provost called to confirm Bret's support for appointing one of the engineering technology departments chairs as interim dean of the new college. It was only with this phone call that Bret began to realize the extent of the work that was necessary to reorganize. It meant, at the very least, splitting off two departments (along with their administrators, faculty, staff, students, space, and finances) and housing them in three new departments in their "new" college [Structural & Human Resource]. Nineteen months may sound like a lot of lead-time, but placed on top of regular decanal job, time evaporated.

Other complications arose that were not anticipated. For instance, the College of Science and Technology was named in an endowment. Which college would receive the endowment? What parts of it? The college's centralized advisement center was now to be divided. Which college would receive how many staff, and which ones? What was an acceptable process for these decisions that would stand up to the scrutiny of faculty, staff, students, and the provost? Much guesswork ensued. Bret did not know of deans who had gone through a similar situation, and there was no resource book for guidance.

Against Bret's recommendation, the endowment was moved to the new engineering college. The interim dean argued successfully that this move was in line with donor intent. And although he was probably correct, the move negatively impacted several initiatives in Bret's college that supported students and faculty in research and service. A messy debate also occurred over the split of the advisement center. Only new resources added by the provost's office mitigated some of the tension. Wrangling over space continued for several years.

Once the engineering college was implemented and marketed, enrollment in its programs surged, as did the demand for service courses in the science and math departments in the science college. It is unclear, however, how much of the growth can be attributed to the splitting of the college versus to the conversion of engineering programs.

The reorganization in this case was made primarily for symbolic and marketing purposes. This is not an uncommon rationale. We interviewed deans at a range of institutions where this kind of change had occurred, and making STEM-aligned programs stand out from the historical liberal education backdrop of Arts & Sciences was a common driver for change.

Case: Keeping up with the Joneses

In this case, a new president and provost were hired shortly after a campus was upgraded from a community college to a baccalaureate-granting university. The university had three colleges: Arts and Sciences, Business, and a college housing the campus's applied programs. The president declared that to be a legitimate university and not a community college, the campus needed a stand-alone STEM college like other successful universities [Symbolic]. The Arts and Sciences college was divided into three parts: STEM; Social Sciences; Arts & Humanities. New deans were hired as leaders for the new units.

The president's goal was achieved by forming a STEM college that resembled those at other universities he viewed as successful. Two unintended yet positive outcomes were realized. The earlier colleges were organized as historical accumulations of programs and they had become unwieldy over time. With the reorganization, programs were placed into colleges where faculty was better aligned. This realignment made recruiting faculty easier. It was also easier to promote consistent messages about teaching and research. Second, the three new deans hired were all external and brought with them new tactics to motivate their colleges to embrace the reorganization. In other words, leaders with unconstrained vision were hired to guide the transition.

Yet other unintended consequences were not so positive. For example, several faculty members and politically influential chairs believed they would be appointed as deans for the new colleges. When formal searches and external hires occurred instead, these individuals felt overlooked and underappreciated [Human Resource]. They remained in the colleges for the new deans to work with [Political]. This could have been avoided by making clear the full process of how the new colleges would be developed at the onset of the decision. Further, due to the speed of the division of the colleges, new policies and procedures were put into place without significant input from faculty [Structural & Human Resource].

Over the next five years, the colleges operated as established, and the deans regularly tweaked the number of departments relative to number of office staff/associate deans in their respective colleges in ways similar to shifting between divisional or functional associate deans. When enrollment began to decline concurrently with the decline in state support, the deans of the colleges of Social Science and Arts & Humanities left their positions for other opportunities, and a new provost was hired.

The new provost recommended merging the two colleges now lacking deans rationalizing it would save costs and all the faculty from these two colleges were already located in the same building. The STEM college would remain separate, the main driver for the reorganization at the onset. The provost met with the faculty of both colleges simultaneously to walk through her proposal and ensure they had the opportunity to hear the same message and answers to their questions. The merger went ahead with little concern voiced, and an external dean was hired following a search. The interim dean over the merged colleges was stunned and dissatisfied when he was not selected for the deanship post-merger. This individual holds political sway and continues to reside as a faculty member in the merged college [Political].

Although the initial reorganization into three A&S colleges included an attempt to modernize policies, there was not sufficient time or input to do so adequately, so some were not working well. The second reorganization was used as a "clean slate" opportunity for the faculty and new dean to make constructive revisions. The new dean proactively asked the provost for latitude to make administrative and policy changes in the college. This extra room to maneuver reduced political risk for the dean and led to visionary discussions between college leadership and faculty.

Frustration with the administration escalated among faculty and staff, however, because this second reorganization, the merger, occurred so soon after the splitting of their college. Also, the proximity of time of these reorganizational changes was almost impossible to explain to the external (non-academic) community and alumni. What looked like pragmatic decisions internally looked like chaos from the outside, leading to significant time investment in repeatedly explaining and justifying these changes to the institution's stakeholders [Political].

A merger following a splitting so quickly might seem unexpected. Yet reorganizing after a recent reorganization is not at all uncommon. We interviewed other deans about similar experiences and we researched other cases. Campus leadership changes and pressures on institutions evolves. There are no guidelines—research-based or rules of thumb—on the timing between college reshuffling events. We would hope that given the time investment needed to reorganize, campus leaders are doing this in this institution's best interests and not their own.

Additional cases

The above cases show that splitting can occur from the desire to demonstrate that an institution values specific programs or to appear more like peer (or aspirational) institutions. However, other reasons for splitting exist (see Table 7.2.A at end of the chapter), a few of which are demonstrated in the brief cases below.

University budget model. Just like the Department of Justice breaking up corporate monopolies, some presidents split colleges of Arts and Sciences to increase competition for scarce resources. When a private research university divided A&S into three colleges, it also transitioned to a new budget model that distributed resources according to student credit-hour production. The university stated these new colleges would allow students to select from more core courses more efficiently delivered.

Under this budget model, splitting the liberal arts college has the potential to encourage colleges to offer large sections of relatively unchallenging course work or to encourage the hiring of cheaper contingent faculty. In either case, this could lead to a decline in achievable learning in liberal education courses.

State budget model. With the state poised to change to performance-based budgeting at their public regional university, one president intended to directly pass those budget changes onto the colleges. The president split A&S into two colleges, one being STEM. She anticipated STEM programs would be growing while social science and humanities programs would remain static or even shrink. She wanted to provide the separated STEM college with maximum budget flexibility to support its growth rather than "keeping it financially tied" to programs with a perceived lower potential for growth.

No known reason. At the direction of its new provost, a public research university began discussing dividing the College of Arts and Sciences into three colleges. The provost appointed a task force of faculty to review his recommendation to reorganize, yet surprisingly, never stated his reasoning for proposing this change.

Without a stated rationale, speculation about the basis for reorganization ran rampant. The provost's background seemed to align itself to this recommendation as he had just left the position of dean of a science college at another public research university where Arts and Sciences departments were organized into several discrete colleges. Some believed the move was simply the only way he knew to work with an A&S college. Others thought he was trying to decrease the influence of A&S on campus, while others thought he was trying to increase it. And still others believed it was all just a line for his CV.

Although the task force recommended the college be split, when the task force's report was circulated, the faculty were overwhelmingly against what was viewed as a baseless reorganization that could harm existing interdisciplinary activities and create an excessive amount of work for uncertain gain. The debate dragged on for a year at which point the topic was shelved. The provost did take a few departments from various colleges and place them into a new interdisciplinary college he created, but he accepted a presidency at another institution shortly thereafter.

Merging Two or More Colleges into One

The next examples represent situations when two or more Arts and Sciences colleges are merged into one. The same drivers and processes in these cases may apply when multiple colleges are fused into fewer or when colleges are largely "reshuffled" (where Arts and Sciences programs are moved among colleges to the extent that the colleges are unlike their earlier composition).

Case: Show me the money

Triggered by a large budget shortfall (stemming from both a reduction in state funding per FTE and enrollment declines), the president at a mid-sized, public comprehensive institution announced at a general faculty meeting that the university would merge its four colleges into three colleges to save money and help address the shortfall [Structural].

The president indicated in subsequent discussions that he did not want the administrative load of the deans in the colleges to become so onerous so as to cause them to be ineffective following the merger. He asked deans to consider strategies to keep the number of direct reports to the deans approximately the same as before the merger. The deans initiated discussions with faculty to develop recommendations about how departments could be realigned into fewer units when new colleges were formed.

With no current vacancies in the deanships, one dean needed to return to faculty. At least three of the four deans felt they were likely to be selected to continue. One of the deans—feeling secure in his position—began to speak critically of the merger decision and process. At that point, the president decided to consolidate to just two colleges instead of four, and the "vocal dean" was asked to return to faculty.

With just two colleges remaining in the plan, the division consolidated Arts and Sciences programs into one college and professional programs in the other. The provost appointed deans from among sitting deans without faculty input. Previous faculty feedback and annual evaluations of the deans were used to select the deans best able to help the colleges move through reorganization.

To meet the president's other goal of keeping the number of direct reports to each dean similar to those pre-merger, up to four departments were combined into schools under a single director. Despite being comprised of A&S-aligned programs, one of the newly amalgamated units was assigned to the professional college to balance the loads of the deans.

As the college mergers alone would not save sufficient funds to cover the budget shortfall, the president, provost and deans proactively solicited additional cost-saving suggestions from department chairs and faculty. These suggestions were largely anonymous when they began circulating—despite assurances that they were only suggestions and not plans—the faculty who would be affected (e.g., eliminate program X and its faculty) formed resistance groups and bogged down discussions [Human Resource]. Open fora and meetings with the faculty and student senates were held to try to mitigate these misunderstandings.

Deans were given a target amount of funding to save within their new colleges to help make the budget. Counter to the recommendations of the deans, as former departments were pooled into larger units the president and provost reduced the number of staff in each final unit by at least one and generally more (4 staff to 2, 3 to 1, etc.). Several individuals the deans wanted to appoint as chairs of units rejected the offered positions. Other individuals had to be cajoled into serving.

The dean of the A&S college approached the merger process proactively where possible. She held one-on-one pre-merger meetings with each department chair [Human Resource] and faculty known to be influential among their peers [Political] to learn of their concerns, express empathy, and dispel rumors. The dean believed taking the time to quash rumors in one-on-one conversations was important, because "universities don't run smoothly in the best of times, let alone when the faculty are gorging on gossip."

The dean expedited decisions on programs where faculty would be reduced to meet budget cut goals prior to the reappointment process for faculty, as these faculty could be let go before reappointment, thus minimizing legal risk [Structural]. The dean did not over-promise what structures/practices/programs would be kept as-is, which ensured she could keep her word on the few commitments she did make. She repeatedly emphasized that faculty and staff would not get everything they want, but that the institution would remain strong and employees' new roles would still be enjoyable and manageable.

The dean did not over-promise what structures/practices/programs would be kept as-is, which ensured she could keep her word on the few commitments she did make.

Despite possessing the best of intentions, the dean occasionally internalized negative feelings of others, periodically agreeing verbally with individuals who were espousing anger against the provost/president and the process. She recommends that other deans avoid this trap, as it sets up the dean as a pawn between the faculty and the executive office in future discussions.

When the dean started in her role several years prior, she did not know a lot about college administration. She was overly-cautious and made painful mistakes during her "honeymoon period" with the faculty. Now, as a dean of a new college, she realized she had a second honeymoon with the faculty, while also feeling better equipped with knowledge and experience. She found she could use this time effectively in influencing the direction of the College. (This may be an important consideration as to the placement of a first-time dean or a "repeat" dean into the deanship of a reorganized college.)

Similarly, chairs of departments found unexpected freedom as they rebuilt their units. For example, the new colleges required administrative and physical movement of some programs, providing a chance to realign teaching spaces and teaching/research laboratories without the burden of territoriality established among the pre-merger departments.

The dean also explored the curricula with unit heads for courses that would distinguish a program as distinct from courses which could be taught more generally (e.g., could one applied statistics be taught to all social science majors or did each program need its own statistics course?). Universities are not known for having nimble curricula, so with the course efficiencies they implemented, the dean and unit heads could expand the curriculum for some areas with high student demand.

Although the dean anticipated pushback, the number of people resisting change was in fact higher. Numerous faculty long-known as "team players" resisted the change with arguments that bordered on the ludicrous. The dean reported, for example: "The faculty fought over moving offices. Even when presented with a nicer, larger office, one faculty member argued that she didn't want to move as she 'didn't know how to fill all the space!' While office placement and size as related to the seniority of the faculty had never been raised as an issue, it suddenly became a hot political topic [Political]. Faculty and staff members who were experiencing personal issues outside of their faculty roles felt beleaguered by the change process, and several approached the dean asking if they could be "immune" from the changes given all that was happening in their lives [Human Resource].

To end this case on a positive note, the dean reflected in the following way: "I became a Renaissance dean!" The College roughly doubled in size, providing the dean the chance to meet many new faculty members and broaden her thinking about research, pedagogy, and even students.

Case: 'All in' for administration

A public research university had Arts and Sciences programs divided between two colleges. After several years of service, the president asked most of the deans to come together for a meeting with no stated agenda. Of the two Arts and Sciences colleges, only the dean of the liberal arts college was asked to attend. At the meeting, the president announced he would like to merge the colleges of natural sciences and of liberal arts into a single college. He offered no justification other than that most major research universities have a single college of A&S and this would align them organizationally with their peer/aspirant universities [Symbolic].

The deans present were asked if they supported this concept. Negligible negative feedback was given to the president at the meeting, and with her fellow deans seated around the table, the dean of the liberal arts college was asked to be the dean of the merged college. The president then stated he expected the merger to be completed within one year. The faculty of the colleges were largely against the merger. The faculty had not been consulted, and the dean of the college slated to lose his position to the merger was blindsided.

The president did not offer any convincing rationale and so faculty conjectured additional "justifications": perhaps the merger was envisioned to save some money [Structural], or it may create a more equitable workload/learning environment across undergraduate programs in the new college (since faculty had long been jealous of each other's workloads between the colleges) [Human Resource]. Although the faculty of the liberal arts college met several times to discuss the reorganization and vent their frustrations (with that dean in attendance primarily as a listener), they resigned themselves to the merger and decided to endeavor to make it happen.

Prior to the dean meeting with the president, the dean of liberal arts had been happily leading her college. She had taken the time to build a successful research program prior to becoming dean and she invested in keeping it going. In fact, maintaining an active research program was one of the conditions she negotiated before accepting the deanship. Due to the challenge of being a dean of a combined college of Arts and Sciences, let alone the challenges associated with a getting through a merger not vetted by the faculty, she needed to decide quickly. Would she maintain her research program and step back into her faculty role, or should she give up research and stay on as dean [Human Resource]? She chose the latter option. This scenario is a reminder that deans "serve at the pleasure" of the administration, so job responsibilities can take unexpected turns rapidly. Personal preferences may need to get left behind for decanal duties (and hopefully the greater good of the institution).

This scenario is a reminder that deans "serve at the pleasure" of the administration, so job responsibilities can take unexpected turns rapidly.

The provost appointed an implementation committee comprised of respected faculty from the departments of the two existing colleges [Political]. Several positive outcomes occurred through the work of this committee. Although their actions were focused on the Structural frame, having a faculty committee driving these outcomes also can be viewed through the Political frame of shared governance. First, as the colleges had once been merged several decades previously, the committee took the time to study and understand the problems of being organized as a larger college, and they constructed a plan to overcome those problems. Second, the committee consulted with peers at other merged colleges to find out what worked well and what worked poorly for them. While developing a transition plan, the committee also formulated a strategic plan for the new college that would take advantage of the merger.

Post-merger, the faculty and dean are now discussing how to best organize programs within the College as a collection of schools and departments. This is one of the best approaches we have heard concerning a reorganization. If only every campus were seeded with such proactive faculty!

There was enormous initial frustration from the faculty due to the lack of a clear rationale for the merger. Yet the faculty and dean approached this so constructively and with such positive outcomes resulting that now when asked, the faculty is glad the reorganization occurred.

Through this process, they had met the president's only stated goal of appearing more like the peer and aspirant intuitions he respected. Coincidentally, the single college organization did save some administrative money through the removal of one dean's office (appreciated by the faculty), but one hidden cost was the research agenda/professional expectations of the remaining dean. Upon reflection, if the dean could turn back the clock, she would have strongly advocated that the president make a clear public justification of why this change would be helpful to the institution's faculty and/or students, as this would have helped smooth the transition to acceptance for faculty and even provided the president much desired political cover for making such a decision.

Case: United we stand, divided will follow

From its origin as a teachers college, an institution grew into an eclectic collection of eight colleges, five of which housed Arts and Sciences programs. Reflecting its origins, there were only program coordinators in the colleges and no department chairs, so each dean averaged 100 direct reports including staff and faculty. It was challenging to do anything but manage their reports. Given how busy the deans were with management functions, partnerships among the colleges were limited and faculty resisted change to the status quo.

After several years in the job, the president announced to the university community the eight colleges would be merged into three, and departments would be created [Structural]. Department chairs would serve in limited term appointments so that no individual held power for too long and different faculty would have the opportunity to practice leadership roles [Political & Human Resource]. The president indicated this would be a cost-neutral reorganization, as savings from culling five deans' offices would offset the costs of creating department chairs.

The president appointed a task force to explore other possibilities for reorganization, and the group recommended several different alternatives. Each alternative appeared to minimize the amount of reorganizational change. The president rejected the task force options and imposed the structure he first recommended: departments with term-limited chairs and three new colleges, one of those being a college of Arts and Sciences. The composition of departments in each college was also decided by the president. The new structure would be implemented in less than six months when the new fiscal year began.

Most sitting deans resigned and departed the institution. The provost proposed to have the remaining dean of one of the five liberal arts colleges become the interim dean of the combined A&S college through the reorganization. Faculty expressed concern that the specific dean was an insider to the undesirable change process. The president and provost met with all A&S faculty to assuage their fears [Human Resource]. At the meeting, faculty advanced the name of a faculty member with some administrative experience to serve as interim dean of the combined college in place of the dean recommended by the provost. The provost accepted this recommendation and appointed her as interim dean.

At the same time the reorganization was playing out, the president asked for the university faculty to create new tenure and promotion guidelines to align with the new administrative model [Structural]. Although the tenure and promotion guidelines did need updating, this concurrent request exacerbated faculty fears. Added on top of the reorganization, faculty interpreted the changing policies for tenure and promotion as: "He is trying to get rid of me!" [Human Resource]. Subsequent discussions between the president and the faculty were strained.

During the reorganization, campus leadership changed at a dizzying rate. The provost did not like the new organizational model, so she stepped back to faculty. A search resulted in the hiring of a new provost. Within a few months of her arrival, the president stepped down and left the institution. Despite the president's unexpected departure, the new provost focused on the reorganization and she indicated that the campus was not turning back this far into the process, so the faculty should help her figure out how to do better with this new organization structure. The provost was shortly appointed as president, and another new provost was hired.

To establish the leadership of the new departments, the faculty in each department were asked to nominate their "founding" chairs. In departments where a large majority of faculty were against the merger, the faculty tried more passive approaches to disrupting the reorganization process. Some would not recommend anyone to be chair, others recommended an adjunct or otherwise unviable candidate. The dean indicated that if they would not recommend anyone appropriate for the position then she would be their chair, and "you won't like me as chair." The recalcitrant departments capitulated.

The new president intended to conduct an external search for an A&S dean, but faculty felt it was too daunting of a job given the recent merger of their five colleges into one and the associated unresolved problems. The president agreed to allow the interim dean and provost to split the new Arts and Sciences college into three colleges, with the interim being appointed dean of one of the resulting colleges. Merging the five liberal arts colleges was unpopular, while the splitting of the merged college into three colleges was received favorably among the faculty. The splitting was largely cost-neutral as the merged A&S college had three decanal positions (a dean and two associate deans) so the two associate dean positions were moved to establish a dean's position in each of the new colleges.

From the initial announcement to merge colleges to their subsequent splitting occurred in just three years. Although the president's original goals for the merger were met, the implementation of departments was costlier than the campus community was led to believe. Removing five decanal offices did not cover the costs of establishing 25 departments and decentralized staffing within those units. This led some to mistrust the judgement of the president who initially announced the merger and added to faculty angst. Yet the merger and creation of departments did have beneficial outcomes for the campus as it allowed deans to step into true leadership roles for their colleges and their colleges began to flourish.

Additional cases

The above three cases demonstrate that merging colleges occurs to save money, to look like peers, or to improve the effectiveness of administration. Other reasons for splitting exist (see Table 7.2.B at end of the chapter), a few of which are highlighted below.

Financial exigency. With the termination of many administrators, staff, and faculty, a regional comprehensive campus merged eight colleges into three, with two of the three housing the Arts and Sciences programs. This university was able to meet its reduced budget circumstances when the savings from reorganization were included.

Need for a unified vision. A research university had Arts and Sciences split among three colleges. Through time, the colleges were increasingly in competition with each other for a shrinking pool of funding, resorting to "zero-sum thinking." A new budget model which largely tracked student credit hours was poised for implementation, and there was a widely-held concern that the infighting would make their already insufficient budgets even worse.

The president shared this concern and wanted to find a way to bring the faculty together through a common vision so a new consolidated college could present credible requests for resources to the campus. A faculty task force exploring options noted that the current three-college structure was inadequate to solve their overarching problems. Ultimately the decision was made to merge the three colleges under a single dean to attempt to address these challenges.

Balance political power of colleges. A unionized, mid-sized, comprehensive university had a long-serving president and provost, and was organized into three colleges: Sciences & Social Sciences, Arts & Humanities, and a catch-all professional college. Faculty were concerned that the professional college was becoming financially and politically advantaged over the two liberal arts colleges because of to their non-unified actions. The faculty, however, did not want any deans to lose their jobs. When two of three deans happened to depart their positions, the faculty encouraged the president to form a task force to explore restructuring. The task force drafted several organizational model options and recommended one to the campus.

After extended discussions, the faculty narrowly voted down the proposal (which served as a recommendation to the president), but nonetheless the president elected to reorganize the colleges as recommended. The two liberal arts colleges fused into a single Arts and Sciences college, and the professional college was split into a Business college and a Human Sciences college. The increased size and unified actions of the new A&S college (now by far the largest college) did improve the retention of power and resources in the college to a degree, although some resources continue a lateral move into the professional colleges commensurate with the increasing numbers of students selecting those majors.

For the clear majority of the deans we interviewed, a financial crisis was either the primary reason for college mergers or drove the timing of the merger.

Merging Colleges Across Campuses or Universities

The next examples represent situations when campuses are merged—sometimes called consolidated or unified—and two or more colleges from the different campuses are subsequently merged or significantly reshuffled. These case summaries begin with what led to the merger and then describe the administrative processes and experiences of the college dean(s).

Campus mergers were infrequent in the past but have increased in the past several years. For example, in Georgia alone, both types of mergers have occurred, including mergers of a research university with a comprehensive (Georgia Health Science University and Augusta College), a research university with a community college (Georgia State University and Georgia Perimeter College), two technical campuses (Moultrie Technical College and Southwest Georgia Technical College), and an HBCU and comprehensive campus (Albany State University and Darton State University).

As these Georgia examples illustrate, campuses do not need to be of similar kinds, sizes, or missions to be merged. Private institutions are not immune to consolidation: Philadelphia University and Thomas Jefferson University have merged, as did George Washington University and Corcoran College of Art + Design, and campuses within Hawaii Pacific University (three examples of many).

Case: Rough start, smooth finish

Although separated by a 45-minute drive, two public comprehensives in the same state system were performing well by any measure. A new chancellor of the state system was hired and made a foreshadowing statement, "Why do we need two universities so close together in the same system?" The campuses themselves could easily highlight their distinguishing features: one campus was urban, commuter-based, diverse, and primarily part-time, while the other was rural, residential, less-diverse, and full-time. Surely the chancellor will realize these distinctive characteristics and hence missions?

Shortly after one of the presidents announced his pending retirement, employees of both campuses received an email regarding the imminent merger of both campuses. Everyone from the provosts to the students was shocked. The respective campus presidents soon shared with their campuses what transpired in the lead-up to the announcement. The two presidents had been asked by the chancellor to create a range of options on how the campuses could work together more closely given their proximity. The presidents dutifully created options, from the extremes of sharing a few faculty members to merging the campuses. They expected a protracted conversation on how to grow such partnerships. Instead, the chancellor made the decision immediately and unilaterally.

The faculty divided into two camps. Some opposed to the merger and the opaque process used to get there; they were angry to the point of working with regional newspapers and the AAUP to try and prevent the merger. The other group—even-sized to the first—believed the merger was a good idea. They envisioned a larger campus with more clout in a competitive state system, increased resources, an appearance more like aspirational universities, a wider range of academic programs to which students would have access, and increased research opportunities through new faculty colleagues. This division set the stage for a civil war that utterly divided faculty over the most critical decision of their respective institutions' futures.

Yet, the campuses found pragmatic ways forward to develop trust and appreciation for belonging to a merged institution. Importantly, the system chancellor did not set a deadline for the merger; rather, he allowed the campuses themselves set an appropriate timeline. The faculty senate of each campus was asked to make proposals of how the colleges on each campus could be merged to form new colleges [Structural & Political]. These were proposed as administrative mergers as the faculty were not expected to move between campuses; their college and department administration might be on their campus or the other, however. There were four colleges on one campus and seven on the other; the faculty focused discussion on disciplinary alignment and equity in majors.

The system chancellor did not set a deadline for the merger; rather, he allowed the campuses themselves set an appropriate timeline.

Once the campus senate proposals had been received, multiple open fora were held along with meetings to conduct SWOT analyses (Strengths, Weaknesses Opportunities, and Threats) of the models, faculty were polled, and ultimately the faculty were allowed to vote to select the final composition of colleges. Pre-merger, there were two colleges on each campus housing Arts and Sciences programs. The model voted for by the faculty still had two A&S colleges, one STEM and one humanities and social sciences although each had programs added or subtracted from their former composition.

Initial savings realized across the institutions (several VP offices were combined and administrators and other staff let go) were used to pay faculty for their involvement in any summer work related to the merger process and for all other costs associated with consolidation. Additional funds supported and celebrated new academic and research opportunities between campuses [Symbolic], which capitalized on the benefits of the merger. This immediate re-investment was appreciated by faculty.

Deans were appointed as permanent (with support by acclimation) or as interim through internal searches followed by open searches for permanent deans. A few sitting deans left the institution, while others found internal positions as department chairs.

Although the regents did not impose a timeline, the merger had to be approved by the university's regional accreditation agency, which introduced deadlines. The accreditation agency visited each campus, and the accreditors made it clear they were looking for plans and working documents showing progress and earnest efforts on each campus to make the merger happen.

The dean selected for the unified Humanities & Social Sciences college followed a similar process to develop its structure. At a college retreat, the dean offered a straw model as a starting-point for discussion, and then faculty drafted a model for departments and schools within the college. Multiple programs in a single department (e.g., Department of Physical Sciences with chemistry, geology and physics) potentially could be split into programs within their own department if there were enough faculty and majors from the two campuses to warrant it. The faculty considered department equity in terms of number of faculty, majors, and student credit hours. The faculty from some programs lobbied to be moved to specific departments to help balance the college. This was followed by open fora to discuss the model, surveys, and ultimately a vote to select the final organization of the college. The final vote was in favor of the proposal.

Trying to bring together the cultures of two different campuses was by far the largest challenge for the dean.

While the process (post-announcement of the merger) created strong buy-in for the new institution, challenges did arise. Differences in general education requirements were thought to be easily resolvable because statewide guidelines for general education proficiencies existed that in principle could limit the changes needed between the two institutions. However, one campus used traditional courses to meet these proficiencies (e.g., Introduction to Sociology, Introduction of Psychology) while the other campus had created interdisciplinary courses to do so (e.g., Gender Studies, Sustainability, Global Challenges).

Additionally, distinct college-level general education requirements required resolution. For example, although the A&S colleges on each campus required language proficiency, one accepted American Sign Language (ASL) to meet the requirement while the other campus opposed using ASL to meet the requirement. And each campus had different requirements within their majors, yet there could only be one degree post-merger. Trying to negotiate an "intermediate" degree removed the distinctive nature of the programs each faculty had worked hard to establish. Thus, standardizing course numbering, course pre-requisites, course learning outcomes, program requirements and learning outcomes, all involved facilitation by the dean.

Trying to bring together the cultures of two different campuses was by far the largest challenge for the dean. The campus-based cultural differences informed the differences in their philosophy of general education, college requirements, elective courses in majors, degree requirements, and plans of study for students. Where similar programs existed on both campuses (e.g., BA History), one of the deans had attempted to delegate the discussion of merging the curricula to the faculty of the two units being merged. These cultural differences bogged down conversations in departments.

In retrospect, the dean says he would have helped oversee discussions on general education first and then established some principles for the departments to follow in negotiating changes in their majors prior to delegation [Structural]. Furthermore, he would have started visiting the other campus earlier in the process to begin to establish a presence there and get to know the other faculty and staff earlier in the negotiation process [Human Resource].

Case: Size matters

Less than two weeks before a public announcement, the system chancellor told the presidents of a large regional comprehensive university and a medium-sized, science-focused university that their campuses were to be merged. The primary justifications were that the campuses were located less than a dozen miles apart and efficiencies could be achieved through consolidating administration and redundant science and mathematics programs (these programs were contained in a STEM college on the larger campus and Arts and Sciences at the smaller).

The name of the larger institution and its president were to be retained in the consolidated institution [Structural & Symbolic]. The colleges and deans on the larger campus would remain largely unchanged in structure, but the number of colleges of the unified campus would grow by three. Two colleges would be added that represented concentrations of programs from the smaller campus (engineering and design), and one new college would be created that pulled some programs together from both campuses.

Planning for the merger of all institutional functions began with over fourscore working groups established by the president. The president tasked the academically-focused working groups with deciding how programs would be merged, including where courses, labs, and faculty offices would be located. Few guiding principles were provided to many of the working groups, and many of the recommendations concerning the overlapping STEM programs appeared biased in terms of shifting programs toward the larger campus as few faculty from the larger campus appeared to want to move to the smaller campus.

When the sum of the academic recommendations were explored, if implemented, they would have grown the larger campus by many thousands of students and removed the same number from the already smaller campus. This shift of students and faculty was not practical because both campuses had been growing and were space-limited. Some programs needed to move to the smaller campus. The final decisions on which programs and faculty to move were placed onto the desk of the dean of the STEM college on the larger campus.

The STEM college had five departments before the merger, but one of the departments contained two dissimilar programs and the departments overall were unbalanced in size. Not wanting to lose the opportunity presented by a good crisis, the dean decided to fix the departmental organizational problems as the colleges merged. In agreement with the receiving dean, the department of computer science was moved to be a part of a new college of computer science and software engineering located on the smaller campus. The offices and classrooms of these faculty had to move.

With the merger creating a larger faculty pool supporting each program, the department with unaligned programs was now large enough to justify splitting it into two departments. To achieve relative equality in the number of students and faculty at the two campuses, the dean needed to move the faculty from two additional departments to the smaller campus and the faculty from the remaining departments needed to relocate from the smaller to the larger campus. Like falling dominoes, a chain of office movements was necessary to consolidate the programs on each campus; over 60 percent of faculty from these two colleges were required to move offices. (Imagine the frustration of some of the faculty who now were commuting longer distances from their homes to their place of work [Human Resource]). Furthermore, the consolidated university made the decision to preclude faculty overloads [Structural]. Yet overloads were part of the culture and an expectation of faculty at the smaller campus. This led to further faculty disenchantment.

The dean steered the faculty into and through the tumultuous merger. He made the decision to spend three days a week on the larger campus and the other two on the smaller one. Individual meetings were planned with faculty on the smaller campus to ensure they knew he would listen to their concerns [Human Resource]. He made every effort to be an attentive listener—even at times when the faculty used him as a verbal punching bag. In time, faculty and staff at the smaller campus commented that the dean was the only person who treated them like they were not a burden. The dean encouraged departments to use academic seminars to bring faculty from both campuses together, and the dean held regular college meetings and holiday parties for faculty from both campuses [Symbolic]. The dean established collaborative internal research grants for which faculty from both campuses were required to work together.

It became apparent that university leaders were not aware, at times, of the impact their comments about the reorganization were having at the level of the faculty. For example, a university leader publically commented that faculty would be reimbursed for travel between the two campuses; faculty members were thrilled as this had been a large point of contention with moving offices. However, the dean brought up discretely to the provost that if the colleges needed to pay for such travel reimbursement, they would be beyond bankrupt. In the end, the proposed practice was never implemented. The dean needed to remain proactive in providing such feedback to the provost for her consideration; it was better to catch problems early than deal with the impact as a dean later on.

Leadership at the state and university levels publically announced the success of the merger less than six months after the campuses were joined. Although the dean's efforts helped gain buy-in from faculty, much work remains to be done. The dean and faculty expect it to take 5-7 years to transition to the "new normal."

Additional cases

The two foregoing cases illustrate how merging campuses can be driven by proximity and/or anticipated saving on administrative costs. Merging campuses can also be driven by other factors (see Table 7.2.C at end of the chapter).

Better than the sum of its parts. With no foreshadowing, a state system announced the pending merger of a public research university (graduate medical programs only) with a public master's university (no graduate medical programs). Being public institutions located in the same city seemed to be all they had in common, yet by moving to a common administration, financial efficiencies were possible (redundant presidential and VP offices were eliminated) and a comprehensive research university would result.

However, salary and workloads were highly polarized, and the interim president and all merger committees and processes were led by faculty or administrators from the research institution, garnering little trust of the process at the master's university. The dean of the liberal arts college took on the time-intensive role of "explaining up" to the provost and president topics such as why their tenure and promotion standards did not have the same research standards as the research university faculty; how to recruit non-science undergraduate majors; and what non-science research is and why it is important. This conversation was similar to the type of communication deans use with legislators, but it was not expected this would be necessary internally at the institution.

And then there was this. In the popular press and on social media, a press release wrote of the pending merger of the University of Florida and Florida State University with the goal of creating the largest research university in the nation. This included video footage of interviews with the two presidents discussing the merger. The release was picked up widely and led to much hand-wringing by students and alumni—until everyone realized the date of the press-release was April 1st. It seems even university presidents can occasionally make the time for April Fools shenanigans!

Additional Considerations for Intercampus Mergers

Here is advice and action items suggested by deans who have been through intercampus consolidations. We are not advocating for any particular point of view, but these recommendations served these individual deans well (or would have served them well in hindsight) in the context of their specific intercampus merger.

- Have a plan to address pay differences for faculty from the different campuses who will now be located in the same department.

- Faculty concepts of workloads are likely to be quite different. Discuss with faculty how to unify these expectations when they are housed in the same college/department.

- The academic ability of students and their backgrounds will likely change in the courses taught by faculty. If the perceived quality of students diminishes, remind them to teach to the students they have and not the ones they wish they had.

- Not only is an overall plan needed for the consolidated institution and colleges, plans are needed for departments within the college on each campus to ensure a balance of offices, laboratories and classrooms post-consolidation.

- Numerous additional curricular and policy changes will be required, including ones to standardize course descriptions and learning outcomes; standardize course pre-requisites and how they are enforced; unify general education requirements and unify college-specific degree requirements; create unified degree programs and programs of study; align course numbers; standardize course and program assessments; agree upon data tracking, program modifications, and program directors for accredited programs, and communicate these changes as appropriate to the accreditation agency; and develop new P&T guidelines for the college, then for departments.

- Hold holiday parties and other celebratory events, as these are one of the few activities faculty from both campuses will attend.

An Ideal Sequence for Mandated College Reorganizations

The cases in this chapter demonstrate faculty learn different things at different stages of a reorganization process. The order of such disclosures of information has consequences for the campus and buy-in to the process. Faculty and staff will imagine the worst-case scenario if they lack information they need (e.g., Where will the art program end up? Oh no, will it be merged with accounting because they both start with A?).

Based upon our discussions with deans, and in the ideal situation where all of these factors are controllable by the institution's leadership, we recommend these steps towards reorganization be taken in the following order to minimize employee anxiety (Table 7.1). These are not all of the steps or processes to follow (e.g., whether to appoint or search for a dean, how to use task forces to develop recommendations or make decisions by fiat), just the order of key pieces of the process.

Above all else, no matter what order they decide to follow, campus leaders should remember to be transparent and to publicly present the order and timing of the process(es) that will follow.

TABLE 7.1
Key Steps for Effective Mandated Reorganizations

1. **The president and/or provost should publically state why the existing organizational structure is inadequate to solve the challenges facing the campus or colleges.** The lack of a clear rationale to justify reorganization was the most common complaint of deans interviewed. Knowing why something is worth doing is a big step toward setting a positive tone for reorganization.

2. **The president or provost should state the *general* structure of the reorganized colleges after receiving input from deans and faculty.** Knowing which programs are likely to be housed within each college will begin to address future administrative and academic proximities.

3. **The provost should name the leader of each college.** Faculty, staff and department chairs will want to know who the person who is to lead further changes in the college, even if it is an interim appointment. The president or provost should make it crystal clear to a potential interim and the college faculty what their plans are for leadership in the new unit–via appointments, internal searches, or open searches–to minimize future conflict.

4. **The dean of each college should finalize his or her college structure.** The new leader of each college should have the opportunity to make final adjustments of departmental structure and staffing within the college and to negotiate intercollege exchanges. All faculty and staff members would then know their department chair and dean. The physical location of departments should also be identified (which campus and buildings).

5. **The dean should establish workload assignments.** Deans should establish a college workload policy which should be further defined at the departmental level. This would involve unions or collective bargaining when appropriate. Faculty should be informed of their percentage effort assigned to teaching, research, and service, and which courses they will be assigned to teach. Staff should also have their job descriptions updated to reflect new or revised duties.

6. **The dean should assign faculty and staff physical locations (office, lab, etc.).** If ambiguity existed about where a faculty or staff member's office would be located, now is the time for those decisions to be disclosed, and these placements should logically follow their department and workload assignments.

7. **The dean should initiate a review of the college's policies and procedures for faculty evaluation.** Not immediately developing a unified policy of faculty evaluation for the new organizational structure will leave some ambiguity—and thus anxiety—among faculty members. However, knowing who their boss is, what they will be doing, and where they will be housed are more important for lowering anxiety, which is why these points are found earlier in this prioritized list. Deliberations about how faculty will be evaluated (annually, tenure, and promotion) is dependent upon their workload assignments. Evaluation policies and procedures should be revised the year following the completion of consolidation, so the anxiety of the reorganization itself is not the primary framework for this discussion.

Deans' Recommendations Across Mandated College Reorganizations

When asked what recommendations they would like to make to fellow deans reading this book, the deans we interviewed made the following points. These recommendations are from the context of their campuses; judge which apply to yours.

Re: Communication

- Be transparent in your actions
- If savings are to be had, make it clear to the faculty the process and priorities for reallocating those resources
- Dispel rumors at every opportunity
- Communicate frequently with other deans on campus and your college's faculty senate
- Proactively reach out to key donors to the college and its departments and explain the benefits of the reorganization
- Do not undermine campus leadership in the communication process

Re: Faculty

- Have the process be largely faculty-driven
- You will only prolong the negotiation phase of the merger if faculty are not provided explicit guidance (e.g., the principles to be adhered to in the process)
- If you seek faculty input, let go of your preconceived notions for the outcome and allow the faculty to guide it
- As faculty and chairs like to see they have influenced the result, if you want to provide a straw model so people can understand the concept of reorganization, demonstrate with a model you do not like, as the faculty is certain to recommend something different!

Re: Process

- Define what constitutes a department in collaboration with the faculty and provost, and firmly follow those principles
- Be willing to hire department chairs from the outside depending on the needs of the new unit(s)
- Define in advance how to address organizational changes to named/endowed units (e.g. schools, departments) that may be organizationally moved or modified
- Be solution focused, define the challenges that can be overcome through a new structure, and outline the benefits and the costs that are foreseen, thereby ensuring the time investment and expenditure of political capital will be worth it
- If you are going to reorganize, don't do other major changes at the same time (e.g., Tenure & Promotion changes) and develop post-reorganization priorities for implementation in a prioritized and sequential manner
- As you develop options for reorganization, check with units outside of academic

affairs to see if all the options are technically viable before progressing further (e.g., campus software may limit options available, as can collective bargaining of staff or faculty)

- If you are undergoing a reorganization due to financial or other critical challenges, don't just "rearrange the deck chairs on the Titanic" and do what is necessary to fix the underlying problems
- Expect it to take 3-7 years post-reorganization to settle into a "normal" dean's routine

Re: The Dean

- Do not pretend the problem identified by campus leadership does not exist
- Individuals stepping into an interim dean role during a reorganization process should make it clear to the provost if they are interested in the position as dean of the reorganized college
- College-level reorganizations can rapidly drive down the popularity of a dean; have a 'Plan B' for your career

Summaries of Justifications for Mandated Reorganizations

We hope this chapter provides some insight into the processes used during mandated organizational change of colleges and how deans were involved. To summarize how leaders of universities have stated their case for reorganization, we have outlined those as identified by interviewees under the categories of splitting colleges, merging colleges, and merging campuses in Table 7.2 (p 124).

One common thread among the cases is that most—and sometimes all—of the stated goals of the person driving the reorganization were met following the reorganization. Any politician would be thrilled to have such a track record–and provosts, presidents, and regents are certainly in political positions and are similarly driven toward ensuring positive outcomes. But the bar to demonstrate success is often set so low that the reorganization is virtually guaranteed to be a success by such measures.

The questions that really should be asked are ones that relate to whether the benefits of the reorganization outweigh the costs of morale, lost time on mission related items (instruction, research, and service/extension), and student success. In Table 7.2, it is notable that some of the justifications for splitting and merging colleges are the exact same, and others are quite similar. For example, campus leaders have split colleges to look more like their peers while others have merged them for the same reason. Does looking more like a peer really advantage the institution in any measureable way? Given the institution's history, programs, and context, there may in fact be great reasons why it is good to be organized differently.

Splitting a college has been argued as a mechanism to save funds, either by introducing competition or by purposefully isolating growing programs to spur their further growth. However, letting colleges "fight" over general education credits

TABLE 7.2

Publicly Stated Justifications for Reorganizing Colleges and Campuses

A) Stated Reasons for Splitting Colleges

- Heighten visibility of specific programs at the university
- Increase entrepreneurial opportunities for colleges
- Save funds by increasing competition (hence efficiency) among colleges
- Look more like our peer/aspirant institutions
- Break from teachers college/community college legacy
- Ensure not just one college is committed to liberal education
- Increase the number of administrative voices representing liberal education
- Provide more leadership opportunities on campus
- Create a more equitable workload among campus deans
- Increase interdisciplinary opportunities through clustering similar programs
- Provide deans more time for leadership

B) Stated Reasons for Merging Colleges

- Save funds by reducing the number of administrative and staff positions
- Timing is right as there were one or more open dean positions
- Increase interdisciplinary opportunities through larger boundary crossings
- Look more like our peer/aspirant institutions
- Increase the power of the administrative voice representing liberal education
- Increase budget flexibility for long-term planning by the college
- Place all liberal education programs together
- Create more equitable faculty workloads
- Make liberal education programs more competitive with professional colleges
- Create common vision for liberal education
- Make one college responsible for ensuring complex learning (problem-solving) by students
- Reduce faculty fighting among colleges for limited resources
- Break up college territoriality

C) Stated Reasons for Merging Colleges from Different Campuses

- Centralize administrative functions thereby improving the quality of service and/or saving funds through reducing administrative and staff positions
- Due to declining enrollments/prediction of declining enrollments
- There are more campuses than necessary to serve citizens of the state; need to reduce program duplication in geographic areas
- Distance between campuses is too small to justify separate administrations
- Increase continuation of two-year students into four-year degree programs
- Build a more comprehensive institution with increased identity
- Reduce building/deferred maintenance costs by consolidating functions into fewer buildings
- Increase national rankings
- Increase collaboration among similar programs and faculty
- Allow students access to a wider scope of programs
- Improve course scheduling for students

does not incentivize those colleges to offer the highest quality of learning experience nor does purposefully isolating mature or shrinking programs. Both of these types of savings could readily be made by changing the university's internal budgeting model instead.

Similarly, college mergers have been proposed to save funds by reducing administrative or staff positions. Although this may save funding the first year, often at the college level, additional associate/assistant deans and staff members may need to handle the additional load in the unified office. One dean indicated that by the time his college's merger with another campus was completed, $1.2M had been spent for new websites, stationary, business cards, campus signage, building signs, and marketing. Does a merger to save administrative cost achieve its goal? Or, do hidden costs and effort cost more than such a reorganization is worth?

One dean indicated that by the time his college's merger with another campus was completed, $1.2M had been spent for new websites, stationary, business cards, campus signage, building signs, and marketing.

Although never stated as the primary rationale, defending liberal education has been mentioned as an additional justification for splitting colleges or merging them. From some leaders' perspective, by making one college accountable for liberal education (merge) will result in a stronger core program. Alternatively it has been argued that by making multiple colleges responsible for it (split) there will be a greater intercollege buy-in to the purpose of general education. This same type of argument is used for the balance of campus power: does one dean representing the campus's largest college (merge) have more say than multiple deans sitting around the table representing the liberal arts programs (split)?

Surely the accountability for liberal education and the power associated with the programs can be resolved through improved campus communication and even budget models. Are there truly instances where reorganization was necessary to enhance liberal education? Or is it the campus leader was avoiding more difficult conversations, and the defense of liberal education is a convenient cover that is difficult to disprove?

Interdisciplinarity as an argument for reorganization is intriguing. Individuals pushing for reorganization of any type often see it this argument as a surefire way to increase interdisciplinary instruction and research (i.e., "breaking down the silos"). When splitting colleges, it is thought that when faculty from similar programs (e.g., within the social sciences) spend more time with their peers, and the similarity of the programs naturally helps faculty cross their reduced disciplinary boundaries. When merging colleges, it is thought that by bringing more dissimilar programs into contact, larger boundaries will be crossed and novel approaches to interdisciplinary teaching and research will result. Both could be correct. These are just different scales of interdisciplinary interactions. Surely there are ways to lead conversations—or to change policies or reward structures—that have the same result without the turmoil caused by reorganization?

There is a notable lack of research of the non-financial impact of reorganizations. Measures of relative rate of faculty, staff, and/or student departures could be meaningful, as could the assessment of student learning and even research outcomes (grants received, publications) pre-, during, and post-reorganization. Having someone step forward to address these research questions would be welcomed. Until then, campus executives may continue to reorganize their colleges or campuses for inconsequential reasons that move the campus backwards rather than forwards.

We are not trying to refute the need for the reorganization of colleges. Yet, many of the specific drivers for change seem to be achievable through other less-invasive mechanisms. We urge deans and other leaders to challenge themselves and each other to determine if the existing organizational structure is truly inadequate to solve the challenges facing the campus or colleges before reorganization is considered. Being a better communicator or finding ways for others to communicate more effectively seems a whole lot easier.

8

Conclusion

If you want to improve the organization, you have to improve yourself and the organization gets pulled up with you.
— *Indra Nooyi*

It is impressive that as a busy dean you have found the time to read this book. You may be wondering what to do with the concepts and case studies with which you have become familiar, from the reorganization of office staff to departments to the university's entire academic enterprise. We expect you are now considering at least minor adjustments to your college's structure to improve its effectiveness. Such contemplation is worthwhile. As we trust is evident throughout this book, we believe that deans must seek to continually improve their colleges—or they might soon be out of a job. Your newfound knowledge of organizational options for colleges and the approaches others have taken to enable change provides you pathways towards improvement.

Upon reflection, it might seem like college organization should be easier than described in this book. Shouldn't there be a simple recipe to follow for the choice of organization of staff within the office or number of departments within the college based, say, on the number of students and faculty in your college? If only it was that easy!

As the case studies illustrate, a variety of reasons that are other than systematic drive changes. Politics, funding, career-building, and unique intuitional histories are but a few reasons for change that do not fit into any formula. An additional complication unaddressed earlier is how an "ideal dean" would be defined at an institution given the natural tension between the viewpoints of a dean compared to those of faculty. The fulcrum between these viewpoints is different on every campus and helps nudge deans toward different organizational structures, as we will illustrate in the following section.

College Structure Balances the Power of Shared Governance

The following scenario illustrates how the tensions of the imagined "ideal dean" plays a role in the college's organization: If one person as the imaginary ideal dean could do the job of the entire college office, the college hierarchy would be flat.

Everyone would report directly to the dean, resulting in flawless communication. With all faculty members reporting directly to the dean, the dean would have all the knowledge necessary to make fully informed decisions based in shared-governance. The dean would handle everything in the office from answering calls to processing paperwork to devising and enacting a strategy for change using shared governance. In such a scenario, administrative costs are at their lowest.

To optimize the functioning of the dean as the college grows, the cost and bureaucracy associated with the dean's office increases.

No one can match this ideal, but it is similar to Model II as discussed in Chapter 2 when there is a very small dean's office. Yet, as actual workloads are distributed relative to cost, different models of office and college organization emerge. From a dean's viewpoint, time is limited, so the dean wants to spend less time on transactional processes and more on formulating and acting upon strategic decision-making. Additional staff are thus needed to complete the transactional work of the office and more staff are added as the number of transactions increase. Some of the questions that arise are: Should these staff be centralized or decentralized? When should a supervisor and other support staff be added (towards Model V)?

As the higher-level strategy demands of the college grow, the dean adds assistant deans and associate deans to assist with strategizing and managing some office functions (Model I). As more faculty are added, additional supervision and staff support may be needed. The dean may push towards forming schools (a Model I variant). When the responsibilities and tasks become overwhelming, creating a divisional dean model (IVA) or even an executive dean model (IVB) to assist with overseeing large sections of the college may be the best opportunity for the dean to remain focused on leading, rather than on managing, his or her college.

As complexity in the college increases, the dean's ability to be aware of all information decreases. This leads to the need for establishing formal communication processes along with enumerating additional policies and procedures. In short, to optimize the functioning of the dean as the college grows, the cost and bureaucracy associated with the dean's office increases.

Understandably, faculty will push back against what they view as unnecessary increases in administrative staffing and processes. This opposition complicates the structural, HR, and political frames that support the dean's desire to expand. With every staff member or chair position added, faculty can point out that their workloads have increased and that money could have been used to hire more faculty. When administrative positions such as associate department chairs or divisional deans are added, the faculty often feel a step further removed from the dean's office, as there is one more layer to the communication process to reach the dean (or the provost or the president) who can make decisions. It is reasonable from this viewpoint that faculty members prefer administrative costs be kept low as possible and reporting layers minimal.

What organizational model offers you the best value in leadership and management for the price (and bureaucratic red tape) the faculty and you are willing to accept? There is no precise equation for this question. This can only be answered through protracted exploration of data in conversation with the provost, faculty, and other stakeholders. The range of models presented in this book reflects this balance at different colleges, with varying structures needed to balance the cost and power of shared governance as defined at that institution. As you examine the models, you might envision one that you believe is better suited to your needs or the college's needs and you might also perceive why others keep their model in place. Bolman and Deal's (1984) Four Frames rubric is an excellent tool for navigating through the change process. The Four Frames might also point you towards the organizational model best suited to your college at this time.

It is to your advantage to be aware of situations at your university that would suggest a move to a different model might make sense for your college, regardless if that step is toward a more or a less complex model. The examples in this book often focused on moving from a less complex organizational model to a more complex model to encompass growth in a college. In the context where your college is growing, should you be proactively planning a more complex organizational model? Conversely, in some colleges, student credit hours, majors, and faculty are declining. If that is your college's context, should you be proactively exploring a less complex college model? If you are prepared for such a conversation—and even discussing future possibilities with the provost—there is less of a chance that such a decision will be made for you by superiors (e.g., a president combining two shrinking colleges to save on administrative costs or splitting a large growing college due to insufficient leadership for its faculty).

Summary of Key Points Across Chapters

To prepare you to consider what options exist for college organization, we placed many guiding questions and thought exercises throughout the book. The fact that these arose through interviews with multiple deans speaks for itself. Here are some key points and key questions raised in earlier chapters but reiterated again here because they are essential.

- Questions to address early in your process when contemplating structural change:
  - —Why would the college consider reorganizing?
  - —What factors should be considered in a reorganization, and are these adequately exploring the four lenses of the change process?
  - —What process should be followed?
  - —What kind of interaction should a dean have with the provost, decanal staff, and faculty in the exploration stages?

—If we did end up reorganizing, how would success be measured
and recognized?

- It is important to consider if the college is functioning as well as it can in its current configuration. This may be the most critical issue to understand in the functioning of your office. Will improvements be made by changing the people, the structure, or both? If existing positions are filled with the wrong people for your needs as dean, then change the people—not the structure. Due to retirements or other opportunities, the people are destined to change anyway, so do not needlessly change structure around the wrong people. You do not want to propose change only to then have someone else point out to you that the structure is likely fine but one member of the office staff is not performing well.

- If you are new to the dean's position, particularly if you have arrived from outside the university, you should live in your job for a while and think about the types of individuals who could complement your strengths and cover for your weaknesses in the office's assistant/associate dean and staff positions.

- Even with the right people in the office, deans may need to redefine positions and redeploy individuals. Expect internal reorganization to the dean's office to be an ongoing endeavor as opposed to the infrequent-to-rare reorganization of departments or college structure.

- If you suspect it is more than who is staffing specific positions that is driving the need for change in the college, then collect appropriate data so your decisions are based on information, not instinct or bias. Use data to discuss the case with others and continue to build and share data as you communicate the rationale for change. Reorganizations are highly visible, however, so keeping data or reasoning confidential is usually misguided. If the data, your interpretation of the data, or your rationale are not sound, it would be better to learn that earlier in the exploration process. And just because the envisioned reorganization may be a really great idea and easily justifiable, that does not mean that the faculty or other specific stakeholders will buy into the idea. Consider, and have others (including the provost) help you consider, if the improvements from a reorganization outweigh the political effort and time investment needed to steer the process, especially with the expected pushback from stakeholders not in agreement with the proposed change.

- Do not underestimate the amount of time needed to reorganize. Thoughtfully assessing the need for change and then planning for a restructuring can easily take a year. Implementing the change can take an additional year or more. Reorganization is something you commit to and see through to completion as dean. It is not something you begin and then hand off to another dean as you depart the institution for a new position.

- The bulk of the work for reorganization will be structural in nature, but the political frame will also require a significant amount of attention. The political work will be more difficult and time consuming for a dean new to the institution to successfully navigate.

- Communicate, communicate, communicate! Communicate up to the provost, communicate down through chairs, faculty, and staff, communicate with students, and communicate outside to alumni and other appropriate stakeholders. The responsibility for effective communication rests on you as dean. Stakeholders want to hear directly from the driver of this change process. Delegating the communication of such efforts to others is done at your own risk.

- Ensure that a trusting relationship is in place with the provost, and if the stability of the provost is in question (e.g., poor relationship with president, likely looking for other opportunities), make sure a trusting relationship with the president is also in place. If the provost "changes their mind" while a dean is trying to implement change, the political fallout can be devastating politically. If the provost departs in the run-up to reorganization, having an unknown provost enter the process introduces uncertainty. The reorganization can be workable, however, if you have gained the support of the faculty.

~ ~ ~ ~ ~

Our goal with this book has been to add a few new items to your administrative toolkit. This book offers current examples of organizational change—yet higher education continues to evolve, and new drivers for change and options for reorganization arise every day. Decanal colleagues at other institutions remain one of your best resources for current information, guidance, and commiseration. Remember to network with colleagues regularly for current and contextualized information as you make plans to improve the effectiveness of your college. We wish you the best of success with changes you embark upon for the betterment of your college.

Appendix A

Names Used for Colleges/Schools that House the Disciplines within Arts and Sciences

Agriculture and Environmental Science

Applied Sciences and Arts

Architecture, Arts and Humanities

Art, Media, and Design

Arts and Behavioral Sciences

Arts and Communication

Arts and Humanities

Arts and Letters

Arts and Science

Arts and Sciences

Arts, Education, and Sciences

Arts, Humanities and Social Sciences

Arts, Letters and Education

Arts, Media and Communication Arts, Sciences and Letters

Arts, Sciences and Professional Studies

Arts, Social Sciences and Interdisciplinary Studies

Basic and Applied Sciences

Behavioral and Natural Sciences

Behavioral and Social Sciences

Business and Humanities

Business and Social Sciences

Business, Arts, Sciences and Education College

Communication and Education

Communication and the Arts

Communication, Media and the Arts

Computer, Mathematical and Natural Sciences

Economics and Business

Education and Sciences

Education, Arts and Humanities

Engineering and Natural Science

Engineering and Sciences

Engineering, Forestry and Natural Sciences

Engineering, Mathematics and Science

Family, Home and Social Sciences

Fine Arts

Fine Arts and Communication

Fine Arts and Humanities

Geosciences

Health and Behavioral Studies

Health and Human Services

Health Professions and Sciences

Health, Environment, and Science

Health, Science, and Technology

Heath and Sciences

Humanities

Humanities and Behavioral Sciences

Humanities and Fine Arts

Humanities and Public Affairs

Humanities and Sciences

Humanities and Social and Behavioral Sciences

Humanities and Social Science

Humanities and Social Sciences

Humanities and the Arts

Humanities and Theological Studies

Humanities, Arts and Sciences

Humanities, Arts, Social and Behavioral Sciences

Humanities, Education, and Social Sciences

Humanities, Fine and Performing Arts

Humanities, Social Sciences and Arts

Information and Mathematical Sciences

Languages and Communication

Languages, Cultures and World Affairs

Languages, Literature and Social Sciences

Letters and Science

Letters and Sciences

Letters, Arts and Sciences

Letters, Arts and Social Sciences

Liberal and Applied Arts

Liberal and Fine Arts

Liberal Arts and Education

Liberal Arts and Human Sciences

Liberal Arts and Science

Liberal Arts and Sciences

Liberal Arts and Social Sciences

Life Sciences

Mathematical and Natural Sciences

Mathematics and Sciences

Mathematics, Science and Engineering

Mathematics, Science and Technology

Natural and Applied Sciences

Natural and Behavioral Sciences

Natural and Health Sciences

Natural and Health Sciences

Natural and Life Sciences

Natural and Mathematical Sciences

Natural and Social Sciences

Natural Science

Natural Science and Mathematics

Natural Sciences

Natural Sciences and Mathematics

Natural, Applied and Health Sciences

Physical and Math Sciences

Science

Science and Engineering

Science and Health

Science and Mathematics

Science and Technology

Science, Engineering and Agriculture

Science, Engineering and Education

Science, Engineering and Technology

Science, Health and Engineering

Science, Health and Technology

Science, Media Arts and Technology

Science, Technology and Agriculture

Science, Technology, Engineering and Mathematics Sciences

Sciences and Agriculture

Sciences and Arts

Sciences and Health Professions

Sciences and Mathematics

Social and Behavioral Science

Social and Behavioral Sciences

Social and Behavioral Sciences and Social Work Social and Cultural Studies

Social Science

Social Sciences

Social Sciences and Interdisciplinary Studies

Social Sciences and Professional Studies

Social Sciences and Public Affairs

Theology, Arts, and Sciences

SOURCE: CCAS Newsletter, June/July 2014. Vol 28 no 2.

Appendix B

A Checklist of Potential Responsibilities Within a Dean's Office

Area of Responsibility	Locus of Responsibility	Effort &/or Time Commitment
ACADEMIC PROGRAMS & INSTRUCTION	◀ EXTERNAL ———●——— INTERNAL ▶	◀ LIMITED ———●——— EXTENSIVE ▶
Academic program assessment	← ○—○—●—○—○ →	← ○—○—●—○—○ →
Academic program planning/curriculum development	← ○—○—●—○—○ →	← ○—○—○—●—○ →
Program accreditation	← ○—○—●—○—○ →	← ○—○—○—●—○ →
Transfer articulation agreements	← ○—○—●—○—○ →	← ○—○—○—●—○ →
Transfer students	← ○—○—●—○—○ →	← ○—○—○—●—○ →
Course scheduling/demand above the dept. level	← ○—○—●—○—○ →	← ○—○—●—○—○ →
Curriculum changes (incl. proposals for new courses)	← ○—○—●—○—○ →	← ○—○—○—●—○ →
General education oversight	← ○—○—●—○—○ →	← ○—○—●—○—○ →
General education assessment	← ○—○—●—○—○ →	← ○—○—●—○—○ →
Late grades	← ○—○—●—○—○ →	← ○—○—●—○—○ →
ADA accommodations	← ○—○—●—○—○ →	← ○—○—●—○—○ →
Graduate education	← ○—○—●—○—○ →	← ○—○—●—○—○ →
K-12 issues & programs	← ○—○—●—○—○ →	← ○—○—●—○—○ →
Teacher preparation curriculum	← ○—○—●—○—○ →	← ○—○—●—○—○ →
Oversight of online instruction	← ○—○—●—○—○ →	← ○—○—●—○—○ →
International courses	← ○—○—●—○—○ →	← ○—○—●—○—○ →
Study (semester) abroad	← ○—○—●—○—○ →	← ○—○—●—○—○ →
Internships & co-ops	← ○—○—●—○—○ →	← ○—○—●—○—○ →
Alternative instruction modalities	← ○—○—●—○—○ →	← ○—○—●—○—○ →
ADMINISTRATION	◀ EXTERNAL ———●——— INTERNAL ▶	◀ LIMITED ———●——— EXTENSIVE ▶
Department chair rotation (if applicable)	← ○—○—●—○—○ →	← ○—○—●—○—○ →
Endowed chair rotation	← ○—○—●—○—○ →	← ○—○—●—○—○ →
External communications	← ○—○—●—○—○ →	← ○—○—●—○—○ →
Governing Board/Regents relations	← ○—○—●—○—○ →	← ○—○—●—○—○ →
State government relations & advocacy	← ○—○—●—○—○ →	← ○—○—●—○—○ →
Federal government relations & advocacy	← ○—○—●—○—○ →	← ○—○—●—○—○ →
Title IX	← ○—○—●—○—○ →	← ○—○—●—○—○ →
Extension services	← ○—○—●—○—○ →	← ○—○—●—○—○ →
IT infrastructure	← ○—○—●—○—○ →	← ○—○—●—○—○ →
Inventory	← ○—○—●—○—○ →	← ○—○—●—○—○ →

Area of Responsibility	Locus of Responsibility ◀ EXTERNAL —— INTERNAL ▶	Effort &/or Time Commitment ◀ LIMITED —— EXTENSIVE ▶
ADMINISTRATION CONT'D		
Website development	←○—○—●—○—○—○→	←○—○—●—○—○—○→
Website & electronic records security	←○—○—●—○—○—○→	←○—○—●—○—○—○→
ADA compliance (including website)	←○—○—●—○—○—○→	←○—○—●—○—○—○→
Record keeping & access	←○—○—●—○—○—○→	←○—○—●—○—○—○→
Institutional Review Board (IRB)	←○—○—●—○—○—○→	←○—○—●—○—○—○→
Institutional Animal Care & Use Committee (IACUC)	←○—○—●—○—○—○→	←○—○—●—○—○—○→
HIPAA (where applicable)	←○—○—●—○—○—○→	←○—○—●—○—○—○→
FERPA	←○—○—●—○—○—○→	←○—○—●—○—○—○→
Freedom of Information (FOI)/Open records	←○—○—●—○—○—○→	←○—○—●—○—○—○→
Emergency planning/ Continuity of service	←○—○—●—○—○—○→	←○—○—●—○—○—○→
Legal issues & lawsuits	←○—○—●—○—○—○→	←○—○—●—○—○—○→
Repository for college level policies, memos, manuals, etc.	←○—○—●—○—○—○→	←○—○—●—○—○—○→
Professional dev. for new dept. heads/ass./asst. deans	←○—○—●—○—○—○→	←○—○—●—○—○—○→
Mentoring department heads & deans office staff	←○—○—●—○—○—○→	←○—○—●—○—○—○→
Annual reviews of direct reports	←○—○—●—○—○—○→	←○—○—●—○—○—○→
Diversity efforts in recruitment & professional develpmt.	←○—○—●—○—○—○→	←○—○—●—○—○—○→
College level faculty & staff awards	←○—○—●—○—○—○→	←○—○—●—○—○—○→
Organizing appropriate recognition ceremonies & celebrations	←○—○—●—○—○—○→	←○—○—●—○—○—○→
FINANCIAL ADMINISTRATION/PLANNING/BUDGETING	◀ EXTERNAL —— INTERNAL ▶	◀ LIMITED —— EXTENSIVE ▶
Scheduling classrooms	←○—○—●—○—○—○→	←○—○—●—○—○—○→
Information technology	←○—○—●—○—○—○→	←○—○—●—○—○—○→
Classroom technology	←○—○—●—○—○—○→	←○—○—●—○—○—○→
Efficiency of classroom use	←○—○—●—○—○—○→	←○—○—●—○—○—○→
Online software & support	←○—○—●—○—○—○→	←○—○—●—○—○—○→
Managing large equipment repair/replacement	←○—○—●—○—○—○→	←○—○—●—○—○—○→
Managing space allocation	←○—○—●—○—○—○→	←○—○—●—○—○—○→
New construction projects	←○—○—●—○—○—○→	←○—○—●—○—○—○→
Building maintenance	←○—○—●—○—○—○→	←○—○—●—○—○—○→
Building renovations	←○—○—●—○—○—○→	←○—○—●—○—○—○→
Safety inspections/OSHA	←○—○—●—○—○—○→	←○—○—●—○—○—○→
Strategic planning	←○—○—●—○—○—○→	←○—○—●—○—○—○→
Budgeting	←○—○—●—○—○—○→	←○—○—●—○—○—○→
Spending policies on endowments	←○—○—●—○—○—○→	←○—○—●—○—○—○→
Carry-forward limitations	←○—○—●—○—○—○→	←○—○—●—○—○—○→
Merit & cost of living adjustments	←○—○—●—○—○—○→	←○—○—●—○—○—○→

Area of Responsibility	Locus of Responsibility	Effort &/or Time Commitment
DEVELOPMENT	◀ EXTERNAL ——●—— INTERNAL ▶	◀ LIMITED ——●—— EXTENSIVE ▶
Development/fundraising	←○–○–●–○–○→	←○–○–●–○–○→
Annual giving	←○–○–●–○–○→	←○–○–●–○–○→
Major gifts	←○–○–●–○–○→	←○–○–●–○–○→
Estate planning	←○–○–●–○–○→	←○–○–○–●–○→
Stewardship	←○–○–●–○–○→	←○–○–●–○–○→
Alumni relations	←○–○–●–○–○→	←○–○–●–○–○→
Advisory boards	←○–○–●–○–○→	←○–○–●–○–○→
FACULTY AFFAIRS	◀ EXTERNAL ——●—— INTERNAL ▶	◀ LIMITED ——●—— EXTENSIVE ▶
Oversight of faculty search process	←○–○–●–○–○→	←○–○–●–○–○→
Permission to recruit tenure-track/regular faculty	←○–○–●–○–○→	←○–○–●–○–○→
Diversity recruiting & retention efforts	←○–○–●–○–○→	←○–○–●–○–○→
Targeted hiring	←○–○–●–○–○→	←○–○–●–○–○→
Spousal/partner accommodations	←○–○–●–○–○→	←○–○–●–○–○→
Hiring of part-time faculty	←○–○–○–●–○→	←○–○–●–○–○→
Hiring of temporary full-time faculty	←○–○–●–○–○→	←○–○–●–○–○→
Onboarding temporary faculty	←○–○–●–○–○→	←○–○–●–○–○→
Travel approval	←○–○–●–○–○→	←○–○–●–○–○→
Start-up	←○–○–●–○–○→	←○–○–●–○–○→
Faculty mentoring	←○–○–●–○–○→	←○–○–●–○–○→
Faculty 'onboarding'	←○–○–●–○–○→	←○–○–●–○–○→
Post-doc management	←○–○–●–○–○→	←○–○–●–○–○→
Professional development in teaching	←○–○–●–○–○→	←○–○–●–○–○→
Professional developing in research	←○–○–●–○–○→	←○–○–○–●–○→
Faculty evaluations	←○–○–●–○–○→	←○–○–●–○–○→
Faculty governance	←○–○–●–○–○→	←○–○–●–○–○→
Faculty workload	←○–○–○–●–○→	←○–○–●–○–○→
Workload equity	←○–○–●–○–○→	←○–○–●–○–○→
Teaching loads	←○–○–●–○–○→	←○–○–●–○–○→
Sabbaticals	←○–○–●–○–○→	←○–○–○–●–○→
Research & grants, pre-award	←○–○–●–○–○→	←○–○–●–○–○→
Research & grants, post-award	←○–○–●–○–○→	←○–○–○–●–○→
Faculty effort compliance (federal awards)	←○–○–●–○–○→	←○–○–●–○–○→
Faculty personnel problems- substandard performance	←○–○–●–○–○→	←○–○–●–○–○→
Faculty personnel problems- professionalism	←○–○–●–○–○→	←○–○–●–○–○→

Area of Responsibility	Locus of Responsibility (◀EXTERNAL —●— INTERNAL▶)	Effort &/or Time Commitment (◀LIMITED —●— EXTENSIVE▶)
FACULTY AFFAIRS continued		
FMLA	position 3 of 6	position 3 of 6
ADA accommodations	position 3 of 6	position 3 of 6
Counteroffers	position 3 of 6	position 3 of 6
Annual reviews of accomlishments & activity plans	position 4 of 6	position 4 of 6
Retention, tenure & promotion activities	position 4 of 6	position 3 of 6
Post-tenure review	position 3 of 6	position 3 of 6
STAFF		
Recruiting staff	position 3 of 6	position 3 of 6
Managing staff	position 3 of 6	position 3 of 6
Professional development	position 3 of 6	position 3 of 6
Evaluations	position 3 of 6	position 3 of 6
Personnel problems	position 3 of 6	position 4 of 6
Reclassification of positions	position 3 of 6	position 3 of 6
STUDENTS		
Enrollment management	position 3 of 6	position 3 of 6
Admissions & recruitment	position 3 of 6	position 3 of 6
Advising students	position 3 of 6	position 3 of 6
Career counseling	position 4 of 6	position 3 of 6
Career placement	position 3 of 6	position 3 of 6
Honor Code/Code of Conduct	position 3 of 6	position 3 of 6
Living/Learning Communities	position 3 of 6	position 3 of 6
Graduate student professional development	position 3 of 6	position 3 of 6
Student complaints	position 3 of 6	position 4 of 6
Academic issues	position 3 of 6	position 3 of 6
"Student success"	position 3 of 6	position 3 of 6
Diversity efforts in recruiting & retaining students	position 3 of 6	position 3 of 6
Scholarships	position 3 of 6	position 3 of 6

Appendix C
GUIDELINES FOR ADDRESSING MAJOR ISSUES
that may lead to significan organizational changes such as the closure of a school or college or the merger of two or more schools or colleges.

Adopted by the Syracuse University Senate Committee on Academic Affairs, September 19, 2003

The Senate Academic Affairs draws it charge from the University Senate Bylaws, which state the following: "There shall be a Committee on Academic Affairs which shall concern itself with the academic planning process of the University and with the consideration of academic priorities and organization. It shall advise and consult regularly with the Vice Chancellor for Academic Affairs on all matters that it deems appropriate."

Accordingly, the Academic Affairs Committee, in exercising its mandated oversight, provides the following set of guidelines for the consideration of the potentially significant organizational and programmatic changes. These guidelines complement the procedures adopted by the University Board of Trustees on January 12, 1995, " Academic Program Changes and the Board of Trustees." They are based on the recognition that discussions about academic changes often begin under circumstances in which the outcome is not at all clear or pre-determined. Further, they state the Academic Affairs Committee's general expectations for the consideration of such major issues and provide internal procedural guidance for the committee.

Internal Consideration
When confronted with potentially significant threats or opportunities, school or colleges should undertake serious self-study and planning, while simultaneously engaged in candid substantive dialog with the central administration and other interested parties. The self-study and planning process should address questions put to it by the administration as well as those that arise from its own consideration. The process would normally address the administration's expectation of the unit and unit's specific goals and the resources and options available to achieve those goals. An external review, evaluation, or consultation is generally helpful and would normally occur.

Consultation with the Academic Affairs Committee
After the previously described internal consideration has occurred, and when the central administration is considering the initiation of major structural changes or has under consideration several options for interventions, preliminary consultation with the Senate Academic Affairs Committee should occur. This consultation will provide an opportunity for collegial consideration of the question and possibly advice on how to proceed. The goals of such consultation are to examine the academic issues of potential interest to the whole University, consideration of options for achieving the University's goals, and identification of problems as well as further opportunities that may arise.

Proposal for Action
When either the central administration after consultation with the academic unit in question or the academic unit itself has determined upon a course of action, it should present its proposal to the Senate Academic Affairs Committee, together with its rationale and the evidence in support of the proposed action, for the Committee's review and recommendation to the Senate.

Upon receiving such a proposal, the Committee will expect that the two procedures outlined above will have been completed.

An individual or group of individuals who would be directly affected by the initial proposal may request that the Academic Affairs Committee review an alternative to the proposal presented by the central administration or the academic unit. The Committee may agree or decline to review the alternative proposal. If the Committee declines to review the proposal, it will communicate the reasons to the individual(s) who made the proposal.

Having received a proposal for action, the Committee will review it in the manner it deems appropriate. Among its considerations will be that

- the proposal for action is based on a clear academic rationale that is grounded in the institutional plan, priorities, mission or vision;

- the proposal for action clearly addresses student, staff, and faculty needs and concerns;

- all phases of the process allow effective and timely communications with all stakeholders in the unit(s) and other concerned schools and colleges.

In making its recommendation to the Senate, the Committee will work with the Senate Agenda Committee to assure that the following standards are met:

- there is sufficient time for open discussion, reaction from the unit(s) in question, and possibly consultation with stakeholders or others;

- the time for discussion and reaction is relatively brief in order that the period of uncertainty may not be protracted;

- the University Senate takes action on the proposal in a timely manner.

The University Senate will take such action as it sees fit on the Committee's recommendation and communicate its actions to the Chancellor.

Appendix D
CRITERIA AND PROCESS FOR FORMATION OF A SCHOOL
FROM AN EXISTING UNIT WITHIN A COLLEGE AT UMBC

This document establishes the criteria and process for forming a school from an already ex-isting unit (i.e., a program/department) within a college at UMBC, as well as steps to review its progress after formation.

Necessary but not sufficient criteria for establishing a school within a college include the following:

- The school enhances and aligns with UMBC's and the college's capacities to achieve the stated academic mission

- The field is one in which school status is recognized nationally, with a national/international organization of peer schools, with membership and data-sharing for benchmarking and continuous improvement

- The school (typically) receives professional or disciplinary accreditation

- Formation of a school does not unduly burden or adversely impact the performance of the college it resides in or other colleges or units

- The school will be home to multiple academic programs

A school within a college:

- Shall be headed by a director who reports to the dean

- May include additional sub-structures, as approved by the dean (and USM)

The process for establishing a school within a college includes the following steps:

A. Initial consultation with relevant college dean for approval to proceed
   The college dean may consider many factors in determining whether s/he supports the proposal, including, for example:
   o Strategic plan for the school:
   - Planned changes to faculty resources (five year projections);
   - Five-year budget projections (revenue and expenditure detail);
   - Program development and modification plans, if any;
   - Current enrollments in the academic program(s); and
   - Enrollment projections for programs within the new school, if applicable.

B. Process initiation
   o Development of summary concept proposal, including rationale, statement of need and required resources
   o Submit to Council of Deans for feedback

C. Development of a formal proposal including:
   o Basis for the proposal

- Congruence with UMBC's mission and strategic plan

- Objectives of the proposed school, including those related to criteria for establishing a school

- Current enrollment in the academic program(s)

o Statement of expected resource requirements
- Internal funding (includes reallocation of resources if needed)

- External funding and potential sources

o Designation of lines of authority and administrative structure

o Duties and responsibilities of the director

o Letters of support from all affected/related academic units

o Letter of support from the dean of the college

D. Proposal submitted to provost for review and approval to proceed

E. Review process
o Review by Vice President for Administration and Finance

o Approval by UMBC shared governance

- Academic Planning and Budget Committee

- If curriculum is involved, standard internal review procedures shall be invoked

- Faculty Senate

o Approval by provost

o Approval by president

o External review and approval, if required[1]

Progress report after formation of the school

Following establishment of a school within a college, a progress report on it shall be developed by the director and submitted to the dean of the college, no sooner than two years after the school is established and simultaneously with the next Academic Program Review or Year Three Review of the school's programs, as well as five and ten years after establishment of the school. An update of the following information about the school shall be included:

• Strategic plan for the school

---

[1] Establishment of a School within a College does not require approval by USM when the School essentially replaces a departmental administrative structure, though notice should be sent by the Provost to the USM Chancellor (per 9/13/13 advice of Associate Vice Chancellor). If the School will be further organized into additional administrative sub-structures — such as those requiring increased staffing requirements or other increased infrastructure — or if the School is established outside the structure of a College at UMBC, the added administrative structure must be approved by the USM, per Board of Regents policy.

- Planned changes to faculty resources (five year projections)
- Five-year budget projections (revenue and expenditure detail)
- Program development and modification plans, if any
- Enrollment projections for programs within the new school
- Discussion of the impact of establishment of the school, including intended outcomes and any unintended outcomes that may warrant additional or revised planning

The dean of the college will forward the progress reports to the provost with his/her assessment.

---

http://www.usmd.edu/regents/bylaws/SectionIII/III705.html?t=print.php&zoom_highlight=establish+sc hool

Appendix E

MERGER GUIDELINES (from The University of Arizona 2-25-09)

PHASE 1 – PRELIMINARY DISCUSSIONS

Form Leadership Team
Strong leadership is needed to provide guidance and direction though the proposal development phase.

- Develop plan for working together and sharing information
- Identify central contact person for merger

Assess Value of Merger
Completing the recommended analysis of the Strengths, Weaknesses, Opportunities and Threats (SWOT Analysis) will help identify the value of the merger.

- Components of a successful merger include:
  - Directors, department heads, & deans who are willing to lead change and provide administrative support.
  - Benefits of merging can be clearly defined for all units involved.
  - Faculty who are willing to collaborate and explore new directions.
  - Strong leaders who are effective communicators and good listeners.

- Complete a SWOT Analysis to discover new opportunities and manage and eliminate threats related to the merger.

- Outline the Strengths and Weaknesses for each merging unit.

  STRENGTHS:
  - What are the strengths of your current unit? (rankings, grant support, teaching excellence, student success, recruiting – student and faculty, staff quality, campus and national/international reputation)

  WEAKNESSES:
  - Are there weaknesses in faculty and student recruiting and retention, departmental rankings and reputation, etc.

  - Outline the Opportunities and Threats for the new merged unit.

  OPPORTUNITIES:
  - Analyze your strengths and determine if these can be used to create new opportunities.

  - Analyze your weaknesses and look for ways that eliminating them can create opportunities.

  - What new opportunities are available to the merged unit?

  - What will you be able to do in the merged unit that you are not able to do in your separate units?

THREATS:
- What obstacles do you face?

- Are your unit functions changing?

- Are there financial considerations that will be a threat to the merger?

- Can any of the identified weaknesses threaten the merger?

- Develop and clearly define merger goals (i.e. cost savings, new revenue streams, improved rankings, increased grant funding potential, teaching efficiencies, etc.)

Form Committees to Analyze Current Unit Functions

It is recognized that units have different ways of operating which create unique cultures. The leadership team must be aware of these cultural differences and develop mechanisms for addressing issues that arise when integrating these different cultures.

It is strongly recommended that protocols be established for making decisions and resolving problems. Clear communication and use of these protocols will continue the process of building trust and transparency.

- Form committees with members from all merging units

- List processes and functions that are important to each of the merging units and form appropriate committees to work on these functions. (Potential new committees may include:
    - undergrad and grad programs, faculty (promotion and tenure, teaching, workloads, etc.),

    - inventory and facilities, technology,

    - student support (advising, recruitment, etc.), and finance)

    - Identify committee leaders

Since financial issues can be complex, a few additional guidelines are provided here.

- Collect a snapshot of financial data for all units involved at an agreed upon date and format.

    - Request unit budget data from central administration for all units involved. Identify all financial resources and liabilities by funding source (accounts, budget lines, funding for general education, special funding, funding for all employees, including employee types).

    - Include foundation and donor assets as well as other financial data unique to units.

Develop and Implement Communication Plan

Communication needs to happen throughout proposal development and merger implementation. Information will need to be distributed to various people involved in the process at different times.

A clearly defined communication plan is helpful for creating a culture of trust and openness about the merger.

- Identify the modalities to be used to communicate information about the proposed merger. Modalities may include: websites, town hall discussions, e-mail, informal and formal gatherings, retreats, etc.

- Communicate the identified benefits of the proposed merger to groups critical to the success of the units (advisory boards, professional associations, donors, faculty, students, staff, alumni, etc.) and discuss merger plans with next-level administration

- Develop an action plan to handle communication around unexpected events.

Draft Proposal

- Leadership team should meet with committee chairs to analyze all committee reports

- Discussion and resolution of important issues with staff, students, faculty, and upper administration

- Draft the proposal for the merger

Secure Final Approval in all Merging Units

- Receive support from the next level of administration

- Informal support from faculty, staff, students and other groups (outside professional groups, alumni, donors, etc.)

- Formal faculty vote

PHASE 2 – IMPLEMENTATION

Choose Leadership for the Implementation Phase and/or the New Merged Unit

The Proposal Phase leadership may continue to lead the Implementation or new leaders may be needed to guide this phase. These leaders may or may not be the final leaders of the new unit.

- Determine the method to identify the leader in consultation with your next level administrator.

- Determine situations that may require merger assistance from central administration

Create a Timeline for Completion of Implementation

Leadership, in consultation with the merging units, will need to decide which elements can be merged immediately and which areas need to be modified gradually over time-with an agreed upon end date (i.e. new fiscal year, midyear, end of semester, etc.).

Leaders need to be sensitive to the issues of continuing day-to-day business while completing merging functions. Flexibility when dealing with changing workloads, retraining, centralizing functions, moving personnel, etc. will be helpful.

- The timeline for this phase includes due dates for all the functional areas listed here – (definition of mapping for this process and details are listed below)

    – mapping current functions and activities,

– developing new staffing plan,

– evaluating staffing skills,

– defining final organizational structure,

– creating plan for use and maintenance of facilities and equipment,

– developing a plan for resource allocation

Map Current Functions and Activities

The objective of this step is to understand how functions work in each organization, identify the differences, and then to use this data to create unified processes for all of the functions of the new unit.

This is a detailed analysis of each area identified in the proposal phase (undergraduate and graduate programs, faculty (promotion and tenure, teaching, workloads, etc.), inventory and facilities, technology, student support (advising, recruitment, etc.), and finance – add any areas that may have been overlooked previously.

- Identify a coordinator and teams to collect data about faculty, staff, and student functions and processes.

- Identify: inefficiencies in workflow, duplication of effort, differences in required functions for each merging unit, where there are no staff available to perform required functions of the unit, and activities done by staff and faculty that provide little or no value, etc.

Determine the Functions that are Essential/or Smooth Operation of the New Unit

This is an opportunity to think broadly and develop new and better ways to do the work that needs to be done in the new unit. Consider the pros and cons of centralizing various services. Consider all options and look for benefits that will make the new unit stronger.

- Survey members from all units to determine strengths and weaknesses of the current functions. Interview current employees responsible for the process in your unit. Consider future changes in processing within the University (Mosaic)

- Collect benchmarking data; talk to key central administrative areas; research best practices in the field.

- Document the new workflow processes, roles & responsibilities, written policies & procedures as required.

Determine the Skill-Sets of Classified Staff and Appointed Personnel that are Needed to Perform the Essential Functions of the New Unit

It is anticipated that work will be done differently and more efficiently in the new unit. Identify broad-based skill-sets which will support cross-training and allow fewer people to complete the required unit functions.

- Determine the required skills and the number of people needed for the essential functions of the new merged unit.

    – Consult with human resources for assistance in redefining job descriptions

    – Ensure equity in workload and compensation such as number of people supervised, number of people supported, level of support provided to students, faculty, staff; number of grants supported, degree of multi-tasking, etc.

    – Talk to colleagues in other units performing similar tasks and Human Resources to get an idea of staffing solutions across campus

Develop Classified Staff and Appointed Personnel Staffing Plan for the New Unit

At this time, it is important to redefine how work is done in the new unit. As much as possible, focus on determining the ideal type of person and skill-sets needed to perform the work identified as essential for the new unit, independent of existing staff in the current units.

- Develop appropriate job descriptions, classifications, and compensation plans for all positions in the new merged unit.

- Balance the workload between staff members in the new merged unit.

- Determine reporting lines for each position in the new unit.

- Determine worksite locations for all staff.

- Develop training plan for each position in the new unit, if necessary.

- Develop a process for filling the positions (search committee, appointments, etc.).

- Develop agreements between faculty and staff on the level of support for different functions.
    - Address issues of customer service between the merging organizations. (this may be an area of cultural differences)

- Evaluate salary requirements to meet the needs of the new staffing plan.

Evaluate Existing Staff and Skills

This step will allow the leaders to identify existing staff who have the potential to be assets to the new unit.

- Establish a team to evaluate objectively the existing staffing relation to the new staffing plan.

- Review current job descriptions and performance evaluations.

- Conduct interviews with current staff to discuss career goals.

- Talk to current supervisors, co-workers, subordinates.

- Consult with Human Resources if questions arise.

Implement New Staffing Plan

This is a difficult task. Having the right person for the job will be critical to the success of the new unit.

- Decide which current staff personnel:
    - will continue,
    - need additional training, and
    - will leave the new unit.
- Decide what types of new personnel will need to be hired to run the new unit.
- Process terminations
- Complete hiring process

Determine Faculty Responsibilities and Evaluation Processes in the New Unit

This may require considerable discussion and negotiation. The Provost's Office is available to provide facilitation, if needed.

- Refer to data collected earlier concerning promotion and tenure, teaching, workloads, student support, advising, recruitment, graduate student mentoring, research/scholarly /creative work, etc.
- The above issues will need to be discussed and resolved; compensation, teaching load, research/scholarly/creative work, advising, etc.
- Develop appropriate job descriptions, classifications, and compensation for current faculty and new faculty positions in the new unit.

Define Final Organizational Structure and Leadership Roles for New Unit

- Finalize and document the structure of the new unit:
    - Committees, undergrad & grad programs, leadership roles, reporting lines, faculty & staff roles
- Evaluate any remaining isolated programs, committees, functions (anything that doesn't fit into the new unit) and integrate or eliminate.

Create Physical Facility and Equipment Plan

- Establish a committee or person to gather data on space, facilities and equipment
- Conduct an inventory of space and equipment for all elements of the merged unit. Include offices, classrooms, laboratories, storage space, etc. Document the results.
- Develop a mechanism for space allocation and, if appropriate, identify a funding source for relocation and renovations. Discuss the space needs in relation to the new vision.
- Establish policies and procedures related to space and equipment utilization, shared space and equipment (core facilities). Document these policies and procedures.

Develop Resource Plan

- Examine existing resources (money, equipment, space, people)
- Align resources to meet the new staffing requirements, processes and space plans.

- Determine who makes resource decisions. For example, the department head, faculty committee, executive committee, Dean, etc.
- Determine source of funding for administration, faculty, and staff. Review and revise funding policies, such as indirect cost allocation.

Identify Issues that Require Negotiation

In some mergers, individual faculty or whole units may want to move from one college or department into the newly forming unit in another college or department. Some of the merging units will want to relocate near the core of the new unit and will need space in a different location. This will often require negotiations at different levels in the institution.

- Indentify individuals or units that might be appropriate to join your unit and who want to join your new unit. OR Determine whether new space is desirable for the success of the new unit. OR other issues as yet undefined.
- Determine resources that might be available to use in the negotiation (Indirect Cost Recovery funds for some period of time, teaching courses for the previous unit for a few years, exchange ofFTEs between units, old space that could be traded, etc). Most issues will require discussion with the next level of administration and usually will require final approval from the Provost.

Develop a Strategic Plan for the New Merged Unit

- Review existing UA and any existing college strategic planes), Academic Program Reviews, or accreditation reports from merging units
- Create a strategic plan for the new unit

Develop Plan to Measure the Success of the Merger

Evaluate the metrics used previously to assess the value of the merger. Determine if these metrics are sufficient or if new metrics are required to measure success of the merger. Revise and publish the metrics to ensure all staff and faculty understand how success of the new unit will be measured.

Celebrate

Celebrate small successes throughout. Use social events to gather information in a comfortable atmosphere and to make informal announcements about the prowess of the merger. Depending on unit and situation, determine if a final celebration is appropriate at the conclusion of the Implementation Phase

References

Bolman, L. G. and Deal, T. E. 1984. *Modern Approaches to Understanding and Managing Organizations.* Jossey-Bass, San Francisco CA.

Bolman, L. G., and Deal, T. E. 2003. *Reframing Organizations: Artistry, Choice, and Leadership. 3rd ed.* Jossey-Bass, San Francisco CA.

Bolman, L. G., and Deal, T. E. 2010. *Reframing the Path to School Leadership: A Guide for Teachers and Principals. 2nd Ed.* Corwin Press, Thousand Oaks, CA.

Bright, D. F., and Richards, M. P. 2001. *The Academic Deanship: Individual Careers and Institutional Roles.* Jossey-Bass, San Francisco CA.

Buller, J. L. 2014. *Change Leadership in Higher Education: A Practical Guide to Academic Transformation.* Jossey-Bass, San Francisco CA.

Collins, J. C. 2001. *Good to Great: Why Some Companies Make the Leap... and Others Don't.* HarperBusiness, New York NY.

Krahenbuhl, G. S. 2004. *Building the Academic Deanship: Strategies for Success.* Amercian Council on Education/Rowman & Littlefield Publishers, Westport CT.

Mosto, P., and Dorland, D. 2014. *A Toolkit for Deans.* Rowman & Littlefield Publishers, Westport CT.

Roper, S. S. and Deal T. E. 2010. *Peak Performance for Deans and Chairs: Reframing Higher Education's Middle.* Amercian Council on Education/Rowman & Littlefield Publishers, Westport CT.

Standards of Practice: A Self-Assessment Guide for Colleges/Schools of Arts & Sciences. 2013. Council of Colleges of Arts & Sciences, Williamsburg VA. Web. www.ccas.net > Resources > Standards of Practice Last accessed on July 6, 2017.

Acknowledgements

We thank the Board of Directors of CCAS for its encouragement and financial backing of this project; Amber Elaine Cox, CCAS executive director, for her patience and support; and the many deans and provosts who shared their experiences with us that formed the foundation of this book. Jean Pokorny, graphic designer for CCAS, did her usual phenomenal job of making the content look good. Joy A. J. Howard *(http://www.joyajhoward.com)* proved an excellent copy editor. Larry Mullins helped with feedback on early chapter drafts, and Lonna Freshley provided a final proofreading of the text. Bret is grateful to his wife Kay for putting up with the many late nights, weekends, and other moments that came to be occupied with activities related to this book. Anne-Marie, now retired, was able to do most of her work while her husband John was at the office.

About the Authors

BRET S. DANILOWICZ began his career as a faculty member at University College Dublin, Ireland, conducting research in the fields of coral reef ecology & fisheries biology. His slide into administration started in 2000 when he was appointed as associate dean of science at University College Dublin where he served until 2004. From 2004-2006 he served as associate dean of the college of science and technology at Georgia Southern University, moving into the role of dean from 2006-2012. In 2012, he began as dean of Arts & Sciences at Oklahoma State University where he still serves today.

Danilowicz received a BS Biology from Utica College of Syracuse University and a PhD in Zoology from Duke University. After his administrative career started, he began coursework anew and received an MA Education Leadership & Management from the Open University, UK, followed by an MBA from Georgia Southern University. Danilowicz has been an active participant in the Council of Colleges of Arts & Sciences since 2005, serving on the Board of Directors since 2014 and now also serving as treasurer. He lives in Stillwater, Oklahoma, with his wife Kay and the two youngest of their four children.

ANNE-MARIE MCCARTAN recently completed forty years working at the national, state, and institutional levels of higher education. In 2016, she marked ten years as executive director of the Council of Colleges of Arts & Sciences. From 2004 to 2006 she was president of the Northwest Campus of Pima Community College in Tucson, Arizona. Previously, she was provost and dean of the faculty of Richard Bland College of The College of William & Mary. She served the Virginia Community College System from 1993 to 1999 as vice chancellor for academic and research services and one year as interim president of Rappahannock Community College.

A native of Washington state, McCartan received a bachelor's and master's degree from the University of Washington and a doctorate in education from Harvard University. She is the author of *Unexpected Influence: Women Who Helped Shape the Early Community College Movement* (Rowman & Littlefield, 2017) and co-editor (with Carl J. Strikwerda) of *Deans & Development: Making the Case for the Liberal Arts & Sciences* (CCAS, 2014). She resides in Richmond, Virginia, with her husband John Accordino.

Council of Colleges of Arts & Sciences
Who We Are | What We Do

The Council of Colleges of Arts & Sciences (CCAS), founded in 1965, is the only national organization that exclusively serves arts and sciences deans. CCAS represents a network of 800+ deans and 1200+ associate/assistant deans and fosters excellence in colleges and schools of arts & sciences by:

- serving as a forum for the exchange of ideas and information, and for discussing common problems of higher education as these relate to the arts and sciences
- representing the liberal arts and sciences at a national policy-making level
- operating on the core principles of inclusive excellence
- disseminating information essential to the continuing intellectual and educational strength of the arts and sciences
- advocating for the value of the liberal arts and sciences and partners with like-minded institutions to further this message
- supporting efforts to improve the intellectual stature and the public understanding of the arts and sciences
- being focused on the problems, possibilities, and interests of member institutions

Benefits of Membership in CCAS

All arts and/or science decanal staff of a participating college within an institution are eligible for the following benefits:

- a variety of professional-development seminars, workshops, and webinars
- a 'deans only' ListServ for discussion of issues and networking with other Deans, and a ListServ for associate and assistant deans
- an online searchable database (Deans Knowledge Base) of timely presentations, policy statements, ListServ discussions, and other resources
- training workshops for department chairs/heads, either on campus or at a regional location
- a mentoring program for new deans and associate/assistant deans
- discounted registration fees at seminars and the Annual Meeting
- discounted subscription rate for Change Magazine
- participation in both the data collection and receipt of the New Hires Survey report
- bimonthly newsletters
- access to the CCAS membership directory and mailing list for searches, college newsletters, etc.

Join CCAS

If you are considering having your institution join CCAS, please contact the Executive Director of CCAS. Details concerning registration can be found at *www.ccas.net > Join CCAS*